"As Jim Pathfinder Ewing so c... are many ways to perceive we inhabit.' From the sci to a generous sharing of practical exercises, *Dreams* marvellous treasure trove your awareness of infinit ...ential realities and expand your own horizons."
— *Indie Shaman magazine*

"With *Dreams of the Reiki Shaman*, his growing body of work, and his social networking following, Jim PathFinder Ewing may just be the Carlos Castaneda of a new generation."
— *Grace Walsh, Reiki Master Teacher, author of* Divine Arrows: Weaving the Path of Divine Guidance

by the same author

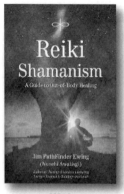

ISBN
978-1-84409-133-1

ISBN
978-1-84409-082-2

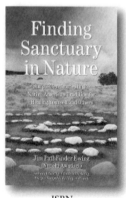

ISBN
978-1-84409-095-2

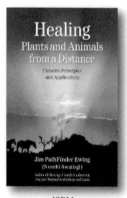

ISBN
978-1-84409-111-9

available from your local bookstore
or directly from www.findhornpress.com

Dreams of the Reiki Shaman

Expanding Your Healing Power

Jim PathFinder Ewing
(Nvnehi Awatisgi)

FINDHORN PRESS

First published by Findhorn Press 2011

ISBN 978-1-84409-568-1

British Library Cataloguing-in-Publication Data.
A catalogue record for this book is available from the British Library.

Edited by Annette Waya Ewing and Nicky Leach
Cover design by Damian Keenan
Illustration by Annette Waya Ewing
Layout by Thierry Bogliolo
Printed and bound in the USA

1 2 3 4 5 6 7 8 9 10 16 15 14 13 12 13 12 11

Published by
Findhorn Press
117-121 High Street
Forres IV36 1AB
Scotland, UK

t +44(0)1309 690582
f +44(0)131 777 2711
e info@findhornpress.com
www.findhornpress.com

To Creator, our guides, angels,
power animals, ancestors, and goddesses,
all good beings of Earth and Sky,
we thank you!

In our world, we are told,
there are people who act
and people who are dreamers of dreams.
Let us be dreamers of dreams
upon which we may act,
and thereby create
a better Dream of the World.

Contents

Preface

This is the fifth book in what has come to be called the PathFinder Series. It deals with environmental shamanism—a way of practicing shamanism that unites us with our surroundings and helps us reconnect to our natural selves. Each of the first four books explores different facets of a way of healing, health, and wholeness applied to the world.

The first three books constitute a trilogy of "people, places, and things" in the shamanic way of viewing the world and all beings. The fourth book, *Reiki Shamanism: A Guide to Out of Body Healing*, combines Reiki with shamanism.

This book expands on that body of knowledge. It focuses on two tools that can dramatically increase the effectiveness of energy medicine practice: recognizing reality in ways that previously, perhaps, had not been fully appreciated—*apprehended*—and seeing that "dreaming," the perception of nonordinary reality, is not limited to the shamanic journey.

This book can be enjoyed as a stand-alone text without having read the previous books, even by those who only have an intellectual interest in the subject matter. My hope is twofold: that practitioners of energy medicine techniques will find that the teachings and exercises in this book expand their horizons and open new doorways to personal growth and development;

and that practitioners of Reiki or shamanism will see that combining the two modalities can dramatically improve their abilities and expand their energetic "tool kit."

Everyone has the ability to journey shamanically, even if it is latent. Having taught students how to journey for many years, I can attest: If you can envision, you can journey; if you can dream at night, you can journey; if you daydream, you can journey. Everyone does it to greater or lesser extent.[1] Follow the instructions in this book and practice the exercises and your own level of understanding will take you where you need to go.

As in previous books, I am not advocating that you reject Western medicine, professing to diagnose any illnesses, or prescribing any cures. I feel that energy medicine is a powerful complement to Western-style medical treatments—not a substitute for them.

The concepts of medicine and healing in energy work and in Native American/Indigenous teachings are very different from those associated with the Western model. In this book, "medicine" is defined as the inherent power within all things. When this power is acknowledged and brought to the fore, healing begins.

Healing is defined as coming into harmony and balance—wholeness. It is a basic premise of energy medicine that the underlying cause of disease is a lack of harmony, or wholeness. Rather than treating symptoms only, energy medicine seeks to address the underlying disturbances in the energy body that cause physical disruption.

Although the teachings in this book include some

information that is in the previous books, I have made a conscious effort to reduce redundancy as much as possible. Some duplication is inevitable. Where one book or another expands more fully on a concept, a footnote is provided, so the reader may refer to that book if interested in further exploring the subject.

On the Structure of the Book

The book is divided into three chapters:

- The first chapter provides an expanded basis for understanding the world around us from a shamanic perspective. It develops the definition of Reiki Shamanism in such a way as to make clear that it is not necessary to take a shamanic journey in order to perceive nonordinary reality; to the contrary: expanded states of consciousness may be experienced through the simple act of perceiving reality in a more open manner.

- The second chapter provides examples of actual shamanic healing journeys drawn from my more than four decades of experience, so that those of you who journey or see in Dreamtime may have reference points from which to learn new techniques or further develop your abilities.

- The third chapter provides observations, lessons, journeys, and practical advice from classes and students' questions over the years, reiterating some issues from previous books and teachings, expanding upon others, and offering new insights.

Included in this book are instructions and exercises to help you develop your capacity for understanding, practicing, and mastering key concepts. You are encouraged to keep a notebook of your own observations to assist you in discovering new avenues for inner discovery; entries from my own notebook are provided as examples.

As with previous books, each chapter is set up for further exploration by offering key words that may be searched on the Internet for greater understanding. You can access the web directly if reading an e-book version and using a smart device. All of my books are currently available in Kindle, Nook, Sony, and iPad readable text.

The book concludes with a glossary of terms specific to energy healing work. In addition, our website Healing the Earth/Ourselves, at

www.blueskywaters.com,

offers books, CDs, tools, and additional reading material that may be ordered by mail or e-mail, as well as information about periodic classes and workshops.

This book is by no means definitive on the subject of shamanism or Reiki. I give examples of various facets of Reiki Shamanism as suggestions, potential directions to follow, or pitfalls to avoid, based on my own experiences and as a gateway for you, the reader, to begin to engage with the concepts. My way of doing things is not the only way; there are many paths to insight and healing through energy medicine's modalities. The purpose of all of my books is to help provide an opening for you to discern your own truth, and ultimately find your own path.

In the old days, the Cherokee medicine people would employ "sacred formulas," that today would be considered "spells," perhaps, or instructions on how to deal with just about any situation that might come up. Handwritten notebooks would be passed down from teacher to student, detailing the sequence of activities and words to sing, along with descriptions of what would be seen.

While nothing in this series includes the sacred formulas entrusted to me (as they would make little sense to someone who is not familiar with Cherokee lore), the substance of what I put forth in these books is similar to such a notebook, with the descriptions, exercises, personal notes, and experiences. After more than 40 years of study, and more than a decade practicing internationally, I have accumulated a lot of notes. These books are, in effect, my sacred formulas that I hand down to those who would read them, with blessings that they be used in a good way.

Not all of you will have a shamanism teacher at hand to help you develop your abilities when they first show themselves. My intention with this book is to offer you a guide that I hope may prove instrumental in changing the way you perceive the world and enhancing your natural healing abilities. May you find many blessings on this path!

Giving Thanks

I am most indebted to the many teachers who have come along the way. They include Sandra Ingerman, who taught me soul retrieval and introduced me to the Foundation for Shamanic Studies; to William Lee Rand, founder of the International Center for Reiki Training, who was a role model and taught me Karuna Reiki; to a host of Native American and indigenous teachers, including Peter Catches, a 38th-generation Lakota spiritual elder, and his wife Cindy, who both have been inspirations and sources of great awe; and Venerable Dhyani Ywahoo, chief of the Green Mountain Band of Ani Yunwiwa (Cherokee) and founder of the Sun-Ray Meditation Society, with her inspiring devotion to peace and establishment of a living, breathing Peace Village.

There are many, many other teachers to thank, too numerous to name. I am grateful to all of my students, and, of course, to readers who have been the source of inspiration and motivation for writing these books. Many thanks, as well, to Ellen Kleiner of Blessingway Writers Services, who helped me get started on the publishing path, and Thierry Bogliolo of Findhorn Press, who took the leap.

Last but not least, I thank my wife, Annette Waya Ewing, for many hours editing manuscripts, offering feedback, illustrating this and other books, and for being an enduring supporter, loving critic, and constant companion.

Introduction

Being a "Reiki Shaman"

"You are what you do."

—PathWays[1]

Ever since I was small child, my dreams were often vehicles for prescience or wisdom expressed in symbolic form. This sometimes made for awkward conversations while I was growing up, because I would be describing things that I "saw" that others could not relate to.

In one recurring dream, I found myself staring up at a deep blue sky with a bright golden sun, and I had to squint my eyes to see. Soon, I saw movement, way above, almost beyond seeing, and kept looking until I saw something spiraling, spiraling, spiraling down, down, down . . . appearing larger and larger, until I made it out: a feather falling to the earth. It landed lightly, right before me.

I picked up the feather and marveled at it—a gift from the sky, a blessing from heaven. As I held it, it turned into something else. Try as I might, I would always awaken not knowing what the feather had become in my hands.

Throughout my life, this dream has "come true" many times. The first time I remember this happening, I was 10 years old. It had snowed. The sky was blue, blue, blue, and cold. The sounds of my footsteps crunching through the frozen crust of deep snow was so loud, it was the only thing I could hear. An icy breeze burned my face.

Suddenly, I thought I heard something else, and looked up. I saw the golden sun in the deep blue sky, and became utterly disoriented, feeling as if I were a feather spiraling to earth. I swayed and struggled to keep my balance, looking down at my feet. There was bright red upon the snow. Blood? Was this one of my nightmares? Of battles, and screams and death? No.

I looked again and remembered being a 10-year-old boy in the yard outside my home. Then I saw the bright red color against the snow was a bird, a cardinal.

I looked at the bird; the bird looked at me. I picked him up, gently, holding him close to my face. In that moment, I knew the dream had meaning; that whenever I needed something in my life, something that was important, I would see the blue sky, and the golden light, and what was needed would appear—even if I didn't recognize the need for that particular thing right then.

The bird was paralyzed with cold, so I took him into the house and slowly warmed him in my hands, nursing him back to health. My dear little cardinal friend lived through the winter, and into the spring, sharing his bright songs. This was my first experience healing with my hands, using the techniques that later I would know as Reiki, and of shamans having such dreams to guide them. A little red bird in the snow taught me this.

We don't know why we have the dreams we do. These blessings from heaven often are inexplicable. But, with time, such dreams of the Reiki shaman can take shape and be understood. What I have learned in nearly 60 years of life is that the world is often not as it appears. "Reality" can be the feather falling from the sky, or we can be the feather falling from the sky. If we pay attention to what we see, we find many miracles unfolding before our very eyes.

Let's get started!

Chapter One

Apprehending Reality

*"Reality is merely an illusion,
albeit a very persistent one."*
— ALBERT EINSTEIN

Everything we see and believe about our world, all that
we consider to be true and real, depends on two factors:
perception and interpretation. At heart, that is what
this book is about. I offer ways to "apprehend," or
detect and comprehend, the nature of reality in
expanding your healing practice through techniques
combining the modalities of Reiki and shamanism to
"see" the world as it really is, composed of infinite
realities.

You may ask: How can "seeing" shamanically help
me "see" the world? I can answer this best by offering
an example:

Some years ago, I had a vision in Dreamtime that the
sun was weeping. In this vision, seen while journeying,
I was in space, and I could feel the power of the sun's
rays, the heat, the exciting energy of golden beams
coming from the sun. But then, I felt a colder energy
that was even more compelling. I saw blue energy,
water, flowing from the face of the sun at the same time

it was bathing me in golden light. The blue rays felt as if they were scraping away built-up angers and resentments, actually pulling out old hurts from deep within and washing them away.

My body was cleansed by those blue rays, and as I looked at the brilliant golden orb of the sun, I saw that the rays were coming from the "eyes" of the sun—two eyes that were weeping. I could feel pain from the eyes of the sun, reflected in my body as the old hurts and accumulations of pain, being washed away by the tears of the sun.

Of course, we know the sun can't "weep," or feel pain, nor can water exist on its surface. What I saw, though, is scientific fact, in part. Spectral lines of water have been proven to flow from sunspots. According to astrophysicists, using sensitive light measuring devices, the phenomenon is readily observable.[1] Scientists cannot explain it, but it's verifiably true.

Which makes more sense: My vision of the sun weeping and being healed by it on an energetic level? Or scientists puzzling over a phenomenon without understanding or finding any significant meaning in what they see? Both are discrete perceptions. Both are "true." I saw water coming from the sun—so did the scientists. This is how "seeing" shamanically can help you "see" the world; reality has many faces.

Many people say they only believe what they can touch or see. However, it is common knowledge that 99.99999+ percent of the atom is open space. Now, think about that for a moment. That's a quantifiable fact. What you touch or see is verifiably . . . nothing.

Truths uncovered by physics last century have yet to

become a part of our everyday reality, so grounded are we in a material worldview. Matter exists as both a wave and a particle; it can both exist and be nonexistent— "wink" in and out of existence. It is known that what is perceived as "real" is actually a disturbance in space—a measurable wrinkle in the energy of space. It's the "wrinkle," or perceived solidness, that differentiates matter from space, which is unseen, unknown, and largely unknowable.

What this means is that what is "really real" turns our operative notions of what is "real" upside down. As it turns out, the science of what is "real" is essentially the same mythos (perception) as that of the shamans, seers, and mystics in indigenous societies for thousands of years.

In the words of quantum mechanics, the vast space between the particles is filled with energy, much more so than what is produced to create a particle. Compare this with the shaman's way of thinking, where every "thing" holds Power (with a capital P, acknowledging its life or life-force energy). Every thing has within it the capacity to be something else, more or less than what it appears. What is unseen can have much more power than what is seen. And *how* something is seen can reveal more about what is seen than the way its appearance is sensed.

Indeed, in both the shaman's and the scientist's way of viewing the world, the unseen is much more real than what is touched and seen. The space between the particles of the atom is filled with Power, or potential. It has more power than the particles it produces because its potential to produce is always greater than what is produced. It can always produce more, whereas what is produced can only return to its wave state, adding even more to the potential to produce.

How "real" is the real world? Infinitely unreal. You could cut an atom in half infinitely and never reduce it down to nothing; yet it is the epitome of nothing. Half of nothing is nothing. Put another way: Half of infinity is infinite. This is the real world, not that which is dimly perceived by the lowest common denominator of perception. How much better—and more accurate—it is to see life as balance and harmony, the world a place where we strive to achieve beauty (in Cherokee, *duyuktv*, or *hozho*, the Beauty Way, among the Navajo or Diné) within our beings; to see, feel, and be harmony, finding balance in each moment.

Our very universe may be "unreal" in the scheme of things, scientifically. A theory called inflation posits that the universe we see is just a small bubble of space-time that got rapidly expanded after the Big Bang. There could be other parts of the cosmos beyond this bubble that we cannot see. In these regions, space-time might be very different, and likely doesn't contain stars and galaxies (which only formed because of the particular density pattern of mass in our bubble). It could include giant, massive structures much larger than anything in our own observable universe.[2]

Even time itself is a matter of perception and interpretation. As every schoolchild knows, time is relative. Large bodies such as the sun actually bend time just as they also bend space. So, time is scalable. The "time" measured for an ant walking along the surface of the earth is not the same "time" as the light of a star bending around the sun.

From such "large" examples all the way down to the nuclear level, it is believed that time is the disturbance (events) around particles. But what may ultimately be the key to time is the ratio between them—the fractals of time sequences.

The term fractal refers to the mathematical objects that show self-similarity at different length scales. It is a geometric pattern repeated at diminishing scales to produce shapes and surfaces that cannot be represented by classical geometry but recreate irregular patterns and structures in nature. Each set or frame is unique, but they are scalable and identical, much as events—time— are represented. That is, if similar ratios of scale are superimposed, it's possible that pathways could exist between them. Time and space could be negotiated (time travel)[3].

Scientists are delving into this theoretical way of manipulating reality, using the principles of quantum mechanics. For example, as reported in *Technology Review*, published by the Massachusetts Institute of Technology (MIT) in Boston, a way has been found to "teleport" energy.[4] Photons, atoms, and ions have been shifted from one location to another, based on the work of Charlie Bennett at IBM's Watson Research Center in New York State; one physicist has worked out how to do it with energy, a technique that has profound implications for the future of physics.

The technique relies on the quantum phenomenon called entanglement, in which two particles share the same existence. This deep connection means that a measurement on one particle immediately influences the other, even though they may be light-years apart. The key, according to this line of research, is to send the information the particles contain instead of the actual particles and ensure that there is a ready supply of particles at the other end to take on their identity[5]—in other words, teleportation. Among those studying this phenomenon, there is a growing sense that the properties that govern the universe are best described not by the laws that govern matter but by the laws that govern information.

Information is the bedrock of sacred ceremony as practiced by indigenous peoples for thousands of years. In indigenous societies, those performing ceremonies take great care to arrange the angles of the wood in a sacred fire, as well as the geometry of the burning coals.[6] This is done so that only those spirits that are invited may enter the sacred space. A ceremonial elder probably would not use the term "fractals" in explaining the great care in practicing sacred geometry in the altar space, nor launch into the quantum theory of entanglement to describe the activities; nevertheless, indigenous practices conform nicely with the theories of modern physics.

Again, what we are talking about here is perception and interpretation. The scientist sees the world of matter as being mostly composed of space from which particles are briefly produced and then disappear, perhaps to reappear somewhere else. There are infinite possibilities in the sequence of events (time/space/ matter). The shaman sees the world as *things that are seen*. This can be seen in the Mexican Toltec way of viewing, for example, which includes the *tonal*, or all that may be touched and measured or known, and the *nagual*, all that is unknown, unknowable, and in potential.[7]

Here the similarity between scientific and shamanic practices diverges slightly. In the scientific way of viewing the world, nothing is "real" unless it can be measured consistently; in the shaman's world, what is immeasurable is more real than consensus reality.

Within this matrix of the known/unknown/ unknowable where infinite possibilities reside, there is a thread of life that exists within all "things." For the shaman, it is the life force within himself or herself that connects and binds. In Cherokee, it is the *nvwati*, (nuh-wat-ee) Spirit, that is *osta*, good; the Good Medicine of Creator within everything. In Reiki, itself a form of shamanism, this thread is called "ki," or life-force energy. It binds every living thing and flows through the seen and the unseen, constantly at hand by merely focusing attention on it.[8]

Physicists have a perception of this energy, though, as they continue to look for a "theory of everything," called the "M Theory." So far, the most they have been able to come up with is an infinite number of universes, or as some relate in layman's terms: God blowing soap bubbles. As Dr. Stephen Hawking wrote in *A Brief History of Time*, the discovery of a unified theory of physics could help us to "know the mind of God."

While many scientists involved in mainstream physics are looking for what is called the "strong force" and the M Theory, some theoretical physicists are looking at what can be proven to explain the anomalies of quantum physics. The strong theory came about because what was didn't add up, so a theoretical force was created ▸ absence. The only rationale for creating or devising the strong force is that there were "holes" in the mathematics of current theories.

Since then, astronomers have documented phenomena called black holes, which explain and validate Einstein's theory of relativity. While this theory is now mainstream, there is an alternate idea circulating. There is a vacuum of sorts that creates a flow through time and space that would explain the anomalies, and also be consistent with what we understand of black holes. That theory is called a "Scaling Law for Organized Matter," which describes matter as inextricably linked to black holes.[9]

In this unified field theory, all matter tends toward singularity, or the infinite. For lack of a better word, since this "vacuum" connects and animates (excites potential in) all matter, it could also be called "ki" – the universal (life) force that binds all things. For the shaman, the explanation of the universe is much simpler to describe: All "things" have life within them; they merely express it in differing ways.

The way of the universe, whether seen by a medicine man or a physicist is much the same: All is energy and patterns of energy, whether appearing in particle or wave or subtle energy we cannot measure. Thought is energy. Intent is energy. Trees, rocks, and grass are energy. Prayer is energy, too. We each are a part of this holographic universe, where everything is connected, and what we do affects everything, even if we don't give our actions, thoughts, or behaviors much attention.

In the realms of physics, cosmology, and pure

mathematics, our greatest minds are forging frontiers that do not separate us from our world but circle back to the ways of the ancestors in seeing the world as one holistic being: The Mind of God.

For example, a retired professor of physics at the University of Oregon's Institute of Theoretical Science, Dr. Amit Goswami, explains that there is a "science within consciousness." This not only includes spirit as a variable but is shifting the paradigm of what makes up the universe from a materialistic worldview. The very existence of God is revealed in the signature of quantum physics, Goswami says, through nonlocal, pervasive access to communication outside of space and time that is mediated by consciousness.[10]

So, what is the right view of the "real" world? Does the sun weep for us with cleansing tears that can by seen by our spirit eyes and heart? Or is this "weeping" instead "sunspots analyzed in the H-band region (5540–6997 cm^{-1}) as viewed with the aid of a new (T = 1800 K) laboratory emission spectrum analysis of water covering 4878–7552 cm^{-1}?

Both are perceptions and interpretations that help us to apprehend reality and comprehend what is real and how we relate to it. Both are equally valid views: the shaman's view is at least 29,500 years older, and the scientific one is more specific and narrowly focused. This doesn't mean the scientific view is not relevant—quite the opposite. We would not have our technological society without it. The shaman's view is more expansive, and can lead to different insights and understandings, and ways of bringing balance and harmony back into the world.

Superstition?
The Case of the Lucky Undershorts

Is legendary basketball star Michael Jordan a shaman? What about Colorado Rockies first baseman Jason Giambi? Both routinely practice what psychologists call "sympathetic magic," an activity shamanic practitioners might call directing their Dream of the World.

According to news reports, for years, Jordan wore the shorts from his national championship–winning days at University of North Carolina under his Chicago Bulls uniform. Other professional athletes carry lucky charms or perform rituals, like bouncing a basketball in certain "special" ways before a free throw or kissing the golf ball before a putt. Giambi has said that he slips on a pair of "lucky" underwear when his batting average falls.[11]

Many discount these practices as superstition, saying random improvement or consistent training accounts for any increased proficiency in athletics, not the lucky rituals. But consistently, scientific studies find that people make their own "luck." They beat the odds of statistical predictability. While the scientific literature seeks to explain increased performance as the result of psychological mechanisms, it can't be denied that these rituals work regardless of the explanations applied to them from the outside.[12]

Lucky, or powerful, clothing is not limited to athletes, of course. Since pre-historical times, seers, visionaries, and medicine people have worn special clothing or used special "power objects" in their rituals.[13]

Behavioral scientists may look at ⁄

influence outcomes through faith as ⁄

People who practice energy medicine, ‥

to understand that the ability to shape reality thiou₀

thoughts, beliefs, and understandings is a basic human function. Our thoughts are energy; the universe is energy; and directing energy creates manifestation through myriad means. In short, our beliefs, attitudes, convictions, and actions create our own "luck."

If this amalgam of belief and action (belief itself is an action) is termed by some as "superstition," so be it. The result is that we *affect* reality through our apprehension of it. That is, we project our consciousness upon what we see, reinforcing our preconceived notions of what constitutes reality.

Allowing Miracles

The great divide between the Western view of the world versus the shamanic/indigenous view is most evident when we consider miracles. In shamanism, miraculous events are not only assumed but expected. Science/logic assumes that the only reality is one that is predictable; anomalies are rejected. If it doesn't exist, or exists only in rare instances, then it's statistically invalid, not part of the expected way the universe operates.

To the indigenous/shamanic view, this is the world turned upside down. What is known and can be known is only a tiny circle of understanding; while what is unknown and cannot be known is infinite. So, every act or event is unique, perfectly capable of exhibiting

ˌraculous outcomes. As is well known in quantum physics, the influence of the observer on the observed can be considerable. If one expects to see sameness and predictability, the likelihood of sameness and predictability is enhanced; while, if one expects to see miracles, the likelihood of miracles is advanced.

The hallmark of medicine people throughout time is their belief in miracles. Medicine people are traditionally considered to be agents of miraculous events. For the shaman, nothing is as it seems. We may see time as measurable, linear, and sequential; but the shaman sees time as circular, overlapping, flexible, even repeatable with infinite possibilities in every moment. This reflects the classic left brain/right brain division within us all.

As Albert Einstein once noted: "The intuitive mind is a sacred gift, and the rational mind is a faithful servant. We have created a society that honors the servant and has forgotten the gift."

In this respect, the Western mind is that of a computer: programmed to exclude, seeing the world in binary terms. Effective? Yes. However, it concentrates perception into a systemic way of excluding much that makes life truly alive, unexpected, unique, and abundant in all its many ways: an incredible, infinite act of creation.

The Observer and the Observed

A book by Giambattisto Vico, entitled *The New Science*, was published in 1725. In it, Vico, a professor of

rhetoric at the University of Naples, argued a
self-evident truth: That the world (reality
depend on observation, (the widely accepted Cartesian
view) since "the mind cannot be a criterion of the mind
itself, still less of other truths. For while the mind
perceives itself, it does not make itself."[14]

Rather than being an observer of reality—Descartes'
description of how the mind discerns the the truth—
the mind discerns the truth through creation. Society,
and our views of reality, including mathematics, Vico
argued, is wholly constructed.

Using Vico's philosophical approach, we can see
immediately the element that was lacking in the
foundation of modern science: the observer as
participant in creation. After a century of quantum
mechanics, we have now come closer to Vico's views,
which were highly unpopular in his lifetime. The
observer's participatory role in shaping what is being
observed is now measurable. As Vico observed in the
18th century, the act of observing is an act of creation
in itself; it cannot help but color what is being
observed. When we take Vico's views into our account
in our modern view of science, whole new worlds
become accessible to us.

Vico argued that imagination, not logic, was our
most direct way of knowing. In common with Carl
Jung and other thinkers who came after him, Vico
asserted that linking consciousness with "poetic
universals" better described the nature of reality and
consciousness, recognizing that previous cultures were
instrumental in defining not only what we decide is
reality but how we do so. Applying pure reason, in the

manner of Rene Descartes, he countered, was to "go mad with the rules of reason, attempting to proceed by a straight line among the tortuosities of life, as though human affairs were not ruled by capriciousness, temerity, opportunity, and chance."[15]

Vico's argument is that we define reality according to loci, or places where we reside and observe, and they then become the foundation for what we deem "the true," and the underlying principle of *sensus communis*, or what is perceived as true, and it is this that comprises our consensus reality or worldview.

Today, it is the more "ancient" view, based on Aristotle and brought forward by Vico through the Enlightenment, that is actually more demonstrably accurate than the Cartesian view. That's because it engages and reflects all of our human faculties, allowing "the true" to emerge from "the certain."

It was a physicist, Albert Einstein, who said: "Imagination is more important than knowledge" and "Everything that can be counted does not necessarily count; everything that counts cannot necessarily be counted." Our intuition, the awareness that comes to the fore to apprehend reality, is never divorced from what is before us.

I envisioned the Sun weeping; it was also "seen" by a scientist using a sophisticated machine. Both accounts are true, subjective, and the same, via different methodologies. Would someone with an even more advanced way of seeing and measuring deem both our observations as lacking somehow? More subjective? Less objective? Quite possibly. Consciousness as defined by information, process, or point of view is the defining factor. But the validity of the various approaches is not altered. All are representations of reality that can be and are conveyed to others to become part of the integrated information of others. The shaman and the scientist are not so far apart.

Seeing the Little People:
Inner Crowdsourcing to Define Reality

In the media world today, crowdsourcing is all the rage. Crowdsourcing is a method of producing content or solutions from a willing audience. For example, in community or citizen journalism, individuals who attend a public meeting might report on the activities via blogs offered on a platform by a media company, rather than the meeting being reported by a paid professional journalist.

More broadly, problems or issues are presented via the media, and willing respondents combine their individual talents and experiences to form a collective intelligence applied to the identified problems and issues for the best community-based decisions. In a less wired society, such solutions were often found in the form of town hall meetings, which still exist in some communities.

The ability to perceive in the real world can be called a form of inner crowdsourcing, with the defining mechanism, perhaps, the ability to "see" nonordinary reality without the use of any drug or outside inducement. To any inquiry regarding "seeing," the question might be not what's really real but "Can you see the Little People?"

Most people ordinarily don't see the Little People, which in different societies have various names, including leprechauns, gnomes, gremlins, sprites, and so on. Native American tribal lore tells of little people who stand 2-3 feet tall. In Cherokee, they are called *Yunwi Tsunsdi.* In the *Song of Hiawatha* by Longfellow, they are referred to as *Puk-Wudjies.* The Little People live in rock caves or a hole in the ground. (The Shaman series of mystery novels by James D. Doss feature a recurring character that is the Ute's version: a *pitukupf,* who lives in an abandoned badger hole at his Aunt Daisy's Spirit Canyon. The little being is utterly believable, and an accurate depiction.)

Little People do not like to be disturbed, but virtually everyone has seen one at some point in his or her life, if only glimpsed, and dismissed. *(Oh, I thought I saw something. Never mind. Or, I thought that bush moved! Or, Huh? A minute ago, I could have sworn I saw. . .)* Often, we'll see something out of the ordinary and be taken aback by what we see, then immediately dismiss it and look again at something nearby that can be explained away.

For example, suppose you are driving along and something catches your attention out of the corner of your eye, and you look at it. You see a large odd-shaped bush, and dismiss it. But after you pass it, and look in your rearview mirror, the "bush" is gone. Or, if you stop and get out, you walk to a bush near what you thought you saw, and say, "Oh, it's only an odd-shaped bush." You have effectively blocked out, or ignored, what was before you, then explained away what you saw to calm the rational mind.

That is the power of the crowdsourcing as a reference for viewing the world—literally, the process of evaluating what is real. It is this subjective and subconscious process of evaluation that is reinforced by the consensus view of reality (a majority of people deciding what is real or not), and choosing to see only what they believe is real, that is called objective reality. Our objective reality is largely determined by our conditioning. Normally, any other views, notions, or observations are subconsciously rejected; indeed, they can't be "seen."

This is where the crowdsourcing comes in. These voices of the authorities—parents, teachers, significant others, best friends, enemies—are what shapes your worldview. The Toltec called it the *metate*, the grinding stone, upon which our worldview is shaped. It is the metaprogrammer that determines what we see and what we don't see, even if what we don't see is directly in front of us.[16] If we want to actually see what is in the world, we must learn to allow voices that see Little People (and other normally unseen phenomenon) into the chorus of the crowd that shapes our view of the world.

This book could be considered one of those voices, if you give it credence. It's up to you to adopt the agreements that authorize your metaprogrammer to "see" beyond the view that it was programmed with since birth (and before that, using racial/cultural memory) and is constantly reinforced by Western society. If you follow the exercises in this book, you will be reprogramming the metaprogrammer, introducing new voices to the crowd of the consensus reality that exists within.

Let's address the car-and-bush analogy again—this time with more commentary.

You are driving along in your car and catch sight of something that appears to be a small tree or bush with, a little person standing in front of it or beside it. Immediately, it becomes "just" a bush or small tree, but for a fleeting moment, you experience three "visions" at the same time: one vision includes the little person, one does not, and one includes the little person superimposed on a bush.

Why is this? Well, your right brain, which sees holistically, is generally submissive to the metaprogrammer, which is a part of the ego/function left brain. The ego, because it is predisposed to "see" material objects and physical threats as a defense system overrides the right brain, which sees everything that is perceptible. This screening of what is seen—or allowed to be seen—by the metaprogrammer goes on, beneath our awareness, in the blink of the eye continuously. In that instant, you can almost hear the conversation taking place:

Left Brain: *Ooops, there's one of those Little People. Checking inventory. No, they don't exist in physical reality. Not a threat. Exclude.*

Right Brain: *Here, Consciousness, I think you should see this. I'm imposing a piggyback on the bush next to it, so the brain can decide.*

Left Brain: *Sorry, Dude! You can have all the fun you want in daydreams and nighttime dreaming, but I'm in charge in the Beta wave state of alertness. Override. No Little People seen!*

As a result, you shake your head and say to yourself, *Did I see what I thought I saw? Nahh!*

So how do you overcome the metaprogrammer? Well, one way is to simply populate the inner crowdsourcing with points of view that allow Little People to be seen. If you were to meditate on them, you would find that when you were growing up all manner of people mentioned them—sometimes jokingly, but often with a hint of their existing in reality—allowing for their possibility.

So, if you reprogram the metaprogrammer, when you are driving down the road, the conversation might shift in the following way:

Left Brain: *There's one of those Little People. Checking inventory. Minimal threat in physical reality, though caution is advised. Allow.*

Right Brain: *Here, Consciousness, let's engage other physical and intuitive perceptual abilities and see what this Little Person has to say.*

Left Brain: *Engaging intuition. Wariness authorized. Allow brain to decide next approach.*

This is reprogramming the metaprogrammer.

If you adopt this point of view in daily life, as you progress, you will allow more voices into the inner crowd that shapes your view of reality. This is what medicine men and women do when evaluating the world; they consciously allow the voices of the ancestors and their teachers to influence how they think about the world, what they see, and what they choose to act upon, rather than relying only on their conditioning.

inner crowdsourcing is done subconsciously—it's called intuition—but many people doubt such personal resources and stuff those impressions back down, often with unintended consequences. It's well known in psychology, as Carl Jung determined, that sublimated impulses can erupt elsewhere, either in sometimes positive fashion, such as synchronicities, or in negative ways, such as creating an active shadow self that causes disruptions in one's life through self-sabotaging behavior.[17] In fact, even if it's not acted upon, our intuition is always with us, and can be a remarkably effective guide, as one of many subliminal processes.

Apprehending the Unique Codes of All Beings

Apprehending the Little People, or seeing without judgment, is a critical task in learning to "see" energetically, or expanding one's practice in energy medicine. In the Native way, it is taught as "seeing through your Spirit eyes," so that ancestors and Power beings can be seen. But there is more to apprehending than only discerning; there is "connecting," as well.

It has been said that the eyes are the "gateways to the soul," and this is true. But the eyes are also a way to connect with the soul of another being. Whenever you come into contact with a living thing, and look directly at it, you are "connecting" on a subliminal level. Not only is your subconscious mind recording the physical

aspects of what is seen—the metaprog
constant "threat assessments" as to demeanor
size, possible next actions, or inclinations—bu .. is also
registering contact points energetically, so that the
being may be recognized in the future. If the being is
friendly, there may be value in keeping in contact and
sharing open lines of communication, which in the
shamanic sense are called "cords."

In the shaman's way of viewing the world, whenever
we "connect" with another being, we issue invisible
cords of energy that connect us. Frequently, when two
people who are in love break apart, one of the most
difficult tasks is to sever those cords. Sometimes, with
unrequited love, for example, the shaman must be
called in to energetically cut these cords (more of this
in the third chapter). These cords are real and they are
binding; they connect to the abdomen and they also
help us "anchor" to our reality.

Whenever there is a major shift in our reality that
could dramatically alter the future, it's often described
as "butterflies" in the stomach. It is actually a
rearranging of the assemblage points: the connections
where these cords attach. We bring into reality our
futures by reeling in these cords from extra
dimensions—lassoing and pulling our futures into
reality. When we leave a reality behind, we often feel it
in the pit of the stomach as a feeling of loss or
emptiness—the cords are detaching, pulling loose.

So, when we "connect" with another being, we are
connecting on an energetic level using these invisible
cords. We also are imprinting upon our subconscious
the unique energetic code that this person/being

carries. As a result, we are in contact with that person whenever we direct our attention toward that person, simply by activating the unique code. Every living being has DNA, the unique code that makes that person; we connect with an energetic imprint of that code contained in the energy through direct attention.

For example, if you gaze upon an eagle, and the eagle "connects" with you, whenever you go outside and think of the eagle, you are connecting with it on a subliminal level. It may even show up whenever you go outside. This is how our power animals appear and give us their insights and understandings: we share our unique codes on a subliminal level, even when we are not consciously seeking them.

When brought into consciousness, you are apprehending the being in the sense of seizing or keeping a portion of that being's essence. It is not a "taking," in that true connection is mutual and given freely; it just happens, without preconception or conscious thought. But once you have connected, you can call this being—whether it be an animal or a person or spirit being, such as a Reiki guide—whenever you desire, even and perhaps especially, as one included in your inner crowdsourcing.

Broadening Our Perceptions

Cultivating the inner crowdsourcing a
guides, angels, power animals, and other noncorporeal
beings into awareness allows you to broaden your
perception of reality and act with mindfulness in any
given situation. It's important that we get to know the
personalities/voices behind our daily, global and
minute worldview, if only to release some of the
excluders—the negative, cynical, and nihilistic
impulses that cause chaos, havoc, destruction, and pain
in the world. Those "demons" exist within everyone. It
is up to us to choose which voices we heed and allow
negative voices to subside.

Only a couple of centuries ago, Westerners were
mindful of miracles. Now, we generally base our
observations of the world as being correct only if they
can be verified by computers, binary analysis, or
rational thinking. The shaman's way may be more
realistic, and real: everything is real.

When the unknowable comes into the knowable, we
become who we were born to be: apprehenders of
reality, the namers of things in this world. Through our
unique ability to give order to chaos through our
thoughts, we are the true children of Earth and Sky
upon this earth: the sons and daughters of the earthly
mother, as our flesh is composed of her flesh, and the
sons and daughters of sky, as the heavenly father
ordains us, giving us spirit and the fire (sacred
medicine) of life. It is our role in life, our soul's purpose,
to order energy and reality to suit our higher purpose,
as co-creators with Creator. This is the Power of being,

ıth its imperative to use this power to help bring order and harmony to this world.

In the rush for progress, Western culture rejected ancient knowledge and wisdom ways, thereby negating half of who and what we are. We are not merely rational machines, but living, breathing beings, with two-sided brains that must be brought into balance. When we do so, we will be able to recognize the world and our place in it: the logical, literal, masculine left brain, and the holistic, conceptual, feminine right brain.

Just as our world physically is out of balance, with the patriarchal way of consuming and destroying the fruits of the Earth Mother, so we are out of balance in our own minds and worldviews, sublimating the maternal, giving, bounteous creation of nonliteral, holistic being. In order to walk in harmony, and be who we were born to be, we must allow a balanced view to come forward.

How we apprehend reality is important. There are many ways to perceive this Dream of the World that we inhabit. Let us instead learn to see with our Spirit eyes, and enjoy what is really real in all its bounteous forms.

Exercise 1: Apprehending Reality with a Stone Person

Work with a stone or other "nonliving" object. I say "nonliving," in that an object someone may think is not living, such as a stone, "holds" its energy more firmly to it than a living item such as a plant or animal. I like to say, "Stones are people, too!" But they are not as directly affected by our perception or interplay of consciousness. Practicing your energy awareness on a fragile living thing could adversely affect it. We must feel the energy (apprehend it) before we direct it (consciously or inadvertently). So a stone would be a more forgiving test subject.

Go to a place where there are small stones, such as gravel beside a road, and find one to work with. Do this mindfully, stating out loud your purpose to the stones, and asking out loud which would like to volunteer. You will suddenly see stones "appear" that seem to have greater energy or luminosity. These are the ones that are volunteering.

Now, go to a quiet place and let the stone speak to you. Sit quietly with the stone either in your open palm or on the floor or ground before you. Stay relaxed but also open and in the moment.

Take a few deep breaths, letting the air go in and out slowly. Ground yourself, feeling your bottom firmly on the floor or ground, and allowing earth energy to come up through you, feeling its comforting effects. Appreciate that energy. It may be a subtle force that you feel, but once you are aware of it, you will be able to tune into it, your breathing slowed and your body comfortable.

Now look at the stone, observing "how" you look at it. Do you feel energy coming from your eyes, directed toward it? Or are you feeling the energy emitting from the stone? Silently ask the stone how it feels. Feel how it responds.

Spend all the time you need; you are in no hurry. Ask it other questions, such as where it has been, what it has seen, does it have any wisdom to share with you? Allow plenty of time for answers. They will come subtly, perhaps slowly, as a fleeting thought or image, or a perception, perhaps a mood. This is the interplay between your consciousness and the stone's consciousness, or wisdom.

Enjoy yourself in doing this. Don't be afraid. Stones are not angry, harsh, or judgmental. They give their energy steadily, freely. They are truly wise. But they are sometimes difficult to fathom. Each has its own "personality," so to speak. For example, some have more healing qualities than others; some have distinct attributes. Allow the stone people to speak to you. Apprehend their messages.

When you are through with the stone, make sure you give it your gratitude. Thank it. Hold it in your left hand and feel the energy of your heart going down through your arm, into your palm, and feeling the warmth. Then, return the stone to the Earth Mother.

Exercise 2: Expanding the Scope of Perception

We are so used to "screening" our perceptions—deciding what is real and what is unreal—that we do so unconsciously. It could prove useful to pay attention to the process of perception with a very simple exercise. Go to a place where vehicles are prevalent, but not ones that travel too swiftly. Perhaps a park or other quiet place near a busy highway where vehicles can be heard approaching from a distance. Take a notebook; find a comfortable spot and sit quietly.

Close your eyes. What do you hear? Can you describe what is making the sounds? As an example: One day, I was sitting in my backyard and I heard a rumbling. I thought it was thunder. Then, I listened more closely, and thought, well, maybe it's a jet plane at a distance. Then, I listened and, no, that wasn't quite it. An 18-wheeler at a distance? No. It wasn't until I heard the sound of the engine go up and down a few times in pitch before I realized that it was the sound of a four-wheeled off-road vehicle slowly rumbling down a hill a few hundred yards from our house. That's a normal sequence of perception: hearing a sound, comparing it to known or remembered sounds until the sound is characterized. But if you keep listening, with the intent of discovering what other sounds are heard, you may be surprised at their variety.

For example, how many birds do you hear? Insects? How many can you identify? Of the vehicle sounds, how many are cars? Trucks? Do you hear trains? Planes? Are there others you cannot identify? What are the sounds between the sounds? For example, unidentified squeaks, hums, low-vibration frequencies that are felt rather than heard? In the early days in America, it was common for people to be able to hear sounds 15, 20, even 30 miles away, because of the low amount of ambient sounds. It was joked among the "mountain men" in the Rockies that if they could hear a gunshot (maybe 30 miles away), then it was "getting too crowded" and was time to move. Nowadays, of course, with so many mechanized devices, the sound of silence can be a luxury.

How many of the sounds you hear are you able to identify? Make a list. You might be surprised at how many distinct sounds you perceive and are able to identify and that you routinely block from attention. Observe the process. Recognizing how and what you perceive is a valuable tool in expanding your perception.

Exercise 3: Cultivate an Inner Crowdsourcing, or "Social Network," of Reiki Guides and Angels

You can cultivate the voices within, that shape your world. If you are one who enjoys social networking on the Internet, consider your guides, angels, power animals, Reiki guides, goddesses, and other ascended beings as allowing you to "friend" them. Imagine them as the photos of favorites on MySpace, Facebook, Ning, Yahoo, or whatever networks you enjoy. Whenever you call to mind your significant power animals, guides, kachinas, angels, and other helper spirits, there they are: their smiling faces greeting you, speaking to you when you "click" on them, or "poke" them with your awareness. Converse with them.

Being a child of the '50s and '60s, I tend to see them stacked atop one another in little boxes, like little TV screens, or like the old *Hollywood Squares* TV show, but infinite in scope. The "boxes" have ancestors going back many generations, stacked deep and out of sight, with a few more trusted ones at the top visible layer, along with the most steadfast guides and teachers. Sometimes, when a voice is heard that has pertinent information to a particular problem or issue, for example, from a past life, that "face" comes forward. This connection to guides, angels, power animals, ancestors, and others, is, of course, just a shorthand way to perceive—and heed—them.

A good way to cultivate this inner crowdsourcing is to call them up before you go to sleep at night. Visualize them before you and ask them to advise you on an issue that is puzzling you. You often will receive conflicting opinions, which is good, and part of the process. It may take awhile—days or weeks—to resolve the issue with a consensus. Or, you could awaken the next day with your answer.

To seek to the truth is to go inward and cultivate the voices of truth that reside within us, in the spaces between thoughts. To seek the serenity of truth, is to hear "the still, small voice" that is within everyone.

How do we silence the inner babble? Simply shrug off the habitual patterns of repetitive and often negative thought, as you observe them. They are just reactive patterns and almost never relevant to the present moment. Promote to the front seats of your inner crowdsourcing those voices of calm and wisdom from your guides. With consistent awareness practice, over time, the old patterns of thought will fade to the back and disappear; the voices of wisdom, discernment, and creative, inquiring ability will have room to come through.

Exercise 4: Seeing Behind the Seen

Go for an awareness walk and allow yourself to "see" what's not there. Consciously set your intention to see everything "unseen" before you. Allow it to come forward. It may be a shimmer over here, or an impression of something that when you turn back to look at it is no longer there. It could be just a "feeling," a perception of something, that comes in sideways to your consciousness: a whisper in your ear, a glimpse of something uncertain, ephemeral. Expand your perception, observe without judgment. You may be surprised at all the little niches and corners of the universe that exist around you all the time, going unnoticed by many.

From The Energy Notebook: Eagle on the Run

As I was on my daily run, I saw the bald eagle that sometimes comes to greet me when I take the route that goes far out into the countryside. Whenever I see the eagle, I reach out and touch it energetically and see where my thoughts go. I did so, and remembered when I first started doing long-distance healing work for people. I couldn't explain "how" I could do it, but I could see the person and would do as my guides told me to do.

Later, I read that some people use photographs for long-distance healing. I toyed with that idea, and back then asked the eagle, one of my power animals, about it. I was

told that in long-distance healing, one d᷈
photographs; the power animal, as a po᷈
universe, can locate anyone, anywhere, any ti.....

As I progressed in my work, it came to me that everyone has a unique code. A power animal can provide it. To connect with someone in Dreamtime, meditation, or the shamanic journey, one has only to connect to the code, like dialing in a phone number. In the old black-and-white movies of the previous century, storylines would sometimes show how practitioners of voodoo would make crude dolls with the intended victim's hair or a fingernail in the doll. It was supposed to be funny, a superstition, but now we know better: DNA from a fingernail clipping can replicate an entire human being: a clone. It is the unique signature of that person. Further, energetically, DNA connects each person with all relatives; so that whenever one is doing this type of work for oneself, one is healing all his/her relatives because the major codes are shared. It's like broadcasting across a band of frequencies that includes many channels.

And it works externally, as well. In the way I was taught, in Cherokee, if you make a promise before the sacred fire, or any pronouncement, then it is so; it is a binding contract with Creator. When one is brought into the tribe, or adopted, in front of the sacred fire, then that person "becomes" one of the people. The sacred fire, which is Creator's fire, changes one's DNA. It binds us to the words we say, the promises/intents we create; our flesh is molded to reflect Creator's will. We are enlisted as co-creators with Creator.

It is a solemn task to do ceremony or take any action or decision before the sacred fire. The fire in our hearts, DNA, is forever changed. So, when we become one with the Eagle, and accept other beings as our equals among the plant and animal nations, it changes us, as well. When we "see" with Spirit eyes—truly apprehend reality—we become different beings. We share a different world whenever we connect with that part of ourselves, rather than when we wear the blinders of the ego mind.

From The Energy Notebook: Two Realities as One

In a dream, the voice of my guide showed me that one's consciousness could be captured by a formula on a page, or a string of letters and numbers. This seemed very similar to the way a computer html address can be "clicked" and turned into a view of a website. Then the guide showed me a string of letters and numbers that when fleshed out described a solid object, a big ball, with little lines on it showing its circumference, and so on. Then, another string of letters and numbers that described a beautiful place by a lake—where I've been many times in Dreamtime. Suddenly, we were sitting there by the lake; I could feel the wind in my hair, smell the slightly fishy odor of water and of greenery, could touch the grass beneath where I was sitting with my fingertips. Then, simultaneously, I was in another place staring at a page with a string of letters and numbers. "Same thing," the guide said. "Now, which is more real? The place that I can see and touch, smell and enjoy? Or the string of letters and numbers that describe every single facet of the place but are not seen, touched, or felt?" They are equally real, of course, only I perceive them differently: in the flesh, albeit in Dreamtime, or on the page. They are two realities that are the same, except in how they are perceived.

One of my teachers, a Native American man, a Lakota, who was taught from birth how to be a medicine man, once showed me this lesson another way. He pulled from his cedar box an eagle feather his father had given to him and asked, "What do you see?" I said, "I see a beautiful feather." He smiled and said, "It is the universe." Then, he turned the feather over, where the color was more drab, and asked the question again, "What do you see?" I said again, "A beautiful feather." He smiled again, and said, "It is the universe. Different views, same thing."

From The Energy Notebook:
Too Precious for Rational Thought

Sometimes when I run, I adhere to a training schedule. Other times, when I decide to be spontaneous, this opening of intent makes room for Spirit to come in and give me a nudge. For example, I decided one day to run as far as I thought I could and still be able to run back, just to see how far that might be. I ran for a little more than two miles when I came upon a home out in country where I heard what sounded like a large guard dog. Not wanting to be chased by the animal, I decided to turn around and go back. As I began trotting back the way I had come, I sensed the dog behind me. I stopped and turned, expecting a big brute, and instead there was a little half-Labrador retriever, half something(s) else, eyeing me suspiciously. "Oh, you're just a little puppy," I said, reaching down to scratch her ears. Indeed, she looked almost identical to a dog I had 30 years before. "You just have a great big old bark, don't you!" I said. She starting wagging her tail, so exuberantly that it waggled her whole body, then she rolled over on her back for me to scratch her tummy, which, of course, I did. I then continued to jog with the dog happily trotting beside me, until about half a mile down the road, I told her, "It's time for you to go home!" She obeyed.

There were immediate lessons in this: Things aren't

always as they seem, fears often turn out to be just fears instead of real danger, and sometimes your intent is to accomplish one thing, but the end is quite another.

After that, every once in a while, I would decide to "run to visit the puppy." And it became a routine. I'd run to the place where the dog lived, give her a big hello and pat, and run back, with her accompanying me part of the way. On days she was not around, I'd presume she was off somewhere with her master and would enjoy the scenery instead.

So, in an effort to be spontaneous, I happened upon a meaningful, heartwarming routine. One that reminds me of all the wonderful dogs I have loved in the past and the joys and poignancy we shared; and also connects me with a new furry friend. If I had adhered only to the proscribed, rational goals of my training schedule, I would have missed out.

Review

Apprehending reality:

- The Western view of the world is tilted toward the rational, literal (left-brained); indigenous/shamanic ways of viewing the world are more holistic, intuitive (right-brained).

- I believe the world is out of balance primarily because the Western worldview has tilted our thoughts and behaviors.

- The basis of the scientific way of viewing reality is that everything is measurable; the indigenous/shamanic view is that all that can be seen and measured is finite and virtually

nonexistent compared to the infinity of p
realities; the observed is always influence(
observer because both are necessary to "exist"; ana
miracles are infinite, though immeasurable.

- The roots of the scientific revolution also included
  using intuition, imagination, and recognizing mass
  unconscious archetypes to perceive "truth," or
  reality.

- The modern definition of consciousness is
  essentially what it does (a system of integrating
  information); the shamanic component of such a
  definition is that what is perceived as reality can be
  greatly expanded beyond the five senses to gather
  information that can be integrated.

- "Apprehending" reality is more than reflecting what
  we "think" we see; instead, it is allowing what we
  see to reveal itself to us and "connecting"
  energetically.

- Inner crowdsourcing is a way to expand
  consciousness that utilizes the natural abilities of
  anyone.

Internet key words: *singularity, unified field theory,
scalable, fractals, Giambattista Vico, consciousness,
reality, tonal and nagual, drug-free shamanism, reiki
shamanism*

Internet references: *"Neo in Matrix Meets Architect and
The Architect's Speech" on YouTube.*

Chapter Two

Journeys and Their Meaning

*"Close your eyes and let your spirit start to soar,
and you'll live as you've never lived before."*
—ERICH FROMM

The shamanic journey is recognized by cultures worldwide in many different ways. The various ways to journey are outlined in many books, and there are devotees of each way. We teach and emphasize using the drum to achieve the shamanic visionary state because it's a simple, natural method that anyone can do. It can be "turned on" simply by the vibrations of the drum, allowing the subconscious or right brain to come forward by lulling the ego mind. Then it can easily by "turned off" by simply sitting up, walking around, and becoming present.[1]

The basics are fairly universal. Nonordinary reality is most often defined in three sections: the lower world, the middle world, and the upper world.

The lower world is where power animals reside. It can appear as anything, but requires going through an underground passage of some sort to an entranceway. It is described in myth and folklore as the place deep within the earth, where other realities can be found. A mythic example of a lower world place is the River Styx, where the dead "cross over," the place where Pluto reigns and Persephone travels to while the energies of the surface are in winter and life is below, and where magical, mystical beings reside. It's going down the rabbit hole in *Through the Looking-Glass*, where everything is topsy-turvy, with its own illogical laws and improbable, though powerful denizens.

The middle world is the "real" world, where we live, but seen through the eyes of nonordinary reality. This is useful in scoping out distant places, doing long-distance healing, and it's great for finding lost glasses or car keys. You can journey to see the plants and animals that share our world, listen to what they have to tell us, perhaps learn their songs and whatever else they may be willing to share, so that we can help and heal them and others. (Communing with plants and animals is more fully explored in my book, *Healing Plants and Animals from a Distance: Curative Principles and Applications*.)[2]

The upper world is where the spirit guides and teachers reside, as well as other dimensions. This is the place, for example, where I go to do energy work with people, and also to find lost soul parts, as discussed later.

As you practice journeying, ask your power animal to take you to these places and become familiar with them. The reason these three levels are nearly universally taught is so that people from diverse backgrounds can converse about them with understanding. Our ways of ordering the universe in our minds can be done in many ways, but without a common framework, it's almost impossible to share knowledge. Seeing the universe as three worlds fits with universal archetypes and allows shared experiences.

One could conceivably, for example, "see" the world as being merely a globe with layers upon it, all one "world" but infinitely "deep," like an onion. Since everything in nonordinary reality is a symbol, anyway, there is no end to the types of realities that can be envisioned or the interpretations put upon them. The more one studies shamanism, the more certain ways of viewing the world become universal, even in diverse portions of the globe. Such teachings are called "core" shamanism and provide a framework for ordering one's seeing.[3]

As the previous chapter outlines, journeying using the drum is just one way to apprehend a facet of reality in its fullness (including nonordinary reality). The aim of the shaman is to use the ability to perceive reality in its truest and/or most efficacious form for performing the functions he or she seeks. To the Reiki shaman, that means allowing healing energies to be expressed in the most direct way. In our practice and teaching, that has been to perform Reiki treatments while in the shamanic state. We will examine some examples of Reiki shamanism to expand healing abilities for various widely used purposes. These case studies are what make up the title of this book: *Dreams of the Reiki Shaman.* They have been modified to retain clients' confidentiality, but are drawn from real life experiences involving real people.

Reiki Healing/Extraction

The most common therapeutic activity of the Reiki shaman is the healing session, which normally includes extraction of negative energies that lead to dis-ease. Negative energies are all around us, both of a low consciousness and those that have no consciousness but are patterns of negativity. A frequently given example is: if you were to inadvertently cut someone off in the traffic, they might direct negative words, gestures, or thoughts in your direction. That expression of negative energy can work its way through the levels of the energy body and over time actually enter the physical body causing imbalances or dis-ease. Negative energies are picked up in everyday living, as one cannot avoid being exposed to people's fear, anger, and insecurities.

A primary goal of the shaman is to be discerning, or impeccable, with his or her energy, knowing how to ground, center, and shield from negative energies in any situation and/or remove them when necessary. When people come for a Reiki treatment, they are suffering from negative energy in the aura that needs to be removed. In Reiki, this procedure is called psychic surgery; in the shamanic tradition, it is called extraction.

In a Reiki treatment, a common method of psychic surgery is to hold the first two fingers of the right hand together to concentrate the energy, then direct energy toward perceived blockages. In the shamanic tradition, a common way of extracting unwanted energies is to pull them out with the hands.

In the Reiki Shaman method, unwanted energies are pulled out and tossed away into nonordinary reality, or toward water. Then Reiki energy is directed to the person, surrounding and filling the spaces where the negative energy was removed. Small Reiki mental/ emotional symbols are energetically implanted, so that any remnants of negativity will be flushed out. More Reiki is then given to elevate the general vibration of the aura. This is routinely done as part of the Reiki healing treatment.

Here's an example of a person needing this, as well as other energetic work, as recorded in notes after being perceived in a shamanic journey. We'll call her Miriam.

Miriam's Journey

Bear took me to the Sky Lodge in the upper world.

Met Miriam's teacher, an old man with a long white beard, and her power animal, a black panther, along the way. They were there to assist in finding soul parts.

We saw seven pieces: four big ones, three small ones. Four felt like newer; maybe early adolescence; three older, young child. . . .

Saw Miriam surrounded by power animals, a menagerie of animals. Couldn't make them out exactly, but knew they were there. But was told she needed another.

Went to the lower world and saw a butterfly teeter-tottering along, up, down, all around. Red-and-black butterfly, touch of yellow on wings. Beautiful. Light. Carefree.

Was told this is a power animal she needs at this time, to follow beauty, allow her wings to unfold. . .

When looking at her aura, saw black, ropy things twining around her chest; saw darkness in left abdomen; bits of ash seemed to be floating around her, spiraling toward her. Needs extraction.

That was all.

Came back.

Needed: Seven soul parts; one power animal; extraction Aho.

Let's look at this journey. First off, this was a "scouting" journey. When a person contacts me for any work, I usually journey to get an idea of what's going on and report back my findings. Then, if the client wants to continue, the treatment is performed.

You will see that I went to my usual spot to await my power animal: my bear. I actually have four main power animals that assist me: Bear, Wolf, Eagle, and Owl. Any one of them could appear at any time I wish to journey, but the bear usually appears, as it is my birth totem, or has been with me since birth, and never strays very far. Wolf usually hangs out on the perimeter of my consciousness, guarding me from outside harm. Eagle can be anywhere and only rarely shows up, usually when it's a very important journey or will have lasting implications for me personally, such as a lesson I need to learn. Owl comes sometimes, more so than the eagle; it is a common power animal for a shaman.

So, I journeyed to my usual spot, which recently has been a bole in a tree near our home, and waited for my bear power animal to appear. If another power animal had arrived, that would have been fine; the one that appears is the one that's volunteering for this journey.

In this case, Bear arrived and we went directly to the Sky Lodge, which is a place in the upper world where I go to do energy work.

Sky Lodge appears to me like a little shack floating in space. Inside is a space that looks like a bathtub with visions in it; I can look into this tub-like space and see whoever it is that I am to work on energetically. I do not see the physical body, only the energy body; it appears essentially as areas of light and dark.

The light areas are essentially the meridians of the body, or energy pathways; the dark areas are areas in which there is nothing of interest for me to view, or areas that need extraction. If it's the former "darkness," it's unremarkable; consider it the fascia that holds the body together: It's neither good nor bad, just fleshy material. But in the latter, a "bad" darkness, it will have a negative feel to it somehow, for example, feeling clammy or "bone cold" or will show something in symbolic form that needs extraction. If it's just a chill feeling, then I know that it needs Reiki and I will use my hands held over the area of the person's energy body in this "tub" to direct Reiki to the area. Sometimes I'll feel the Reiki energy coming from my hands and see the dark area start to lighten up. Other times, I'll feel prompted by that—urged by Reiki guides who are always in attendance when working in the Sky Lodge— to draw Reiki symbols with my fingers over the area.

For example, I might draw small Reiki mental/ emotional symbols over a dark area, followed by the Reiki "power up" symbol over them, and then a long-distance symbol over all. That will ensure that the Reiki treatment keeps on working long after I've finished.

Whatever may be required in the Sky Lodge, I usually end up doing a general Reiki treatment and some form of extraction, even if it's only to put a few Reiki symbols in the aura to raise the energy body's vibration rate and deter negativity.

In Miriam's case, however, I was shown that more was needed: "When looking at her aura, saw black, ropy things twining around her chest; saw darkness in left abdomen; bits of ash seemed to be floating around her, spiraling toward her. Needs extraction."

This told me that she needed more specific work that was more urgent than a mere general extraction. Miriam, it should be noted, was a health care professional who worked in a hospital and was constantly surrounded by sickness, death, and dying. She had picked up a lot of negative patterns of energy in her aura and it showed. Although she was a Reiki Master in her own right, no one had shown her how to do psychic surgery or taught her Reiki Shamanism so that she could see these things. Nor had she been taught to ground, center, and shield herself routinely, particularly in her place of work. She became a student and learned how to implement these changes.

In this case, black ropy things were pulled out and thrown away. She said that she had been experiencing shortness of breath, which she believed was panic attacks, and stress-related abdominal pain. Reiki symbols were energetically implanted and out floated a large, black energy mass, which was pulled away. Often, it's impossible to "pull" dark energy out of the body without disturbing energetic systems that need to be there. A way to easily remove such things is to either hold the hands over the area and allow Reiki to saturate the area or to implant Reiki symbols in the dark area, which was done in this case. The Reiki releases or extricates the negative energy as a mass, which can then be easily removed. This was done in the long-distance journey.

The "bits of ash" that seemed to be floating around her was negative energy that had not yet lodged itself in her physical body but was caught up in her aura. That was gathered and swept away in the shamanic journey, as well. Mental/emotional Reiki symbols were implanted in her aura to reflect away negative energy she encountered. In the treatment journey, it was also noted that she had an accumulation of this type of "ash" or filmy opaqueness in front of her third eye. This was also brushed away, so that she could "see" energetically more clearly. It's important for anyone who practices healing modalities to routinely have extraction performed—once a year, at least. When dealing with people experiencing dis-ease, one confronts negative patterns of energy that can be "sticky" and adhere to the health care provider.

One way to ensure that you keep clear is to always clear yourself of unnecessary energetic and psychic debris after any energy work, or in the case of Miriam, before starting work and after leaving work each day. Smudging with sage or cedar or liquid smudge can clear your aura and protect against negativity. (We recommend Blue Eagle Invocation liquid smudge for those who cannot abide smoke or having an open flame around.) Or, you can draw the Reiki "power up" and mental/emotional symbols on your palms then brush yourself off from head to toe.[4]

Afterward, simply give an affirmation, speaking from your heart to Creator or your higher power and guides, angels, and power animals: "Thank you for removing all footprints and energetic debris from me and (the person, or) anyone I've encountered today, or will encounter." A simple affirmation sets the intent for negative energy and patterns of energy to be repelled.

You will notice from the scouting journey that Miriam had many power animals. People who journey a lot, or are in the healing professions, usually have multiple power animals. Much of the healing work we do is subliminal, and the various power animals assist in guiding people to the right healing professional.

For people with owl or butterfly, as in Miriams's case, it's not just a coincidence that a patient with an owl or butterfly power animal might be led to the hospital where Miriam works. She's a beautiful healer whose energy is a joy to be around, working magic with all those who come into her presence. She just needed to learn a few techniques to keep her aura clear so that she could continue to be a shining beacon of health and wholeness for those who needed her healing touch. The addition of a power animal—in this case, Butterfly—was to help her "lighten up" and not be so dragged down by others' pain and suffering.

It's natural to want to "share the pain," because in our society we believe that to be the way we show compassion; however, it's ultimately damaging to our health and well-being. But you will never be able to feel enough hurt to ease anyone else's pain, to paraphrase Dr. Wayne Dyer. You cannot give if your own basket is empty. While it's important to give to others, as a means of sharing joy, happiness, love, and spiritual development, it's also important to keep our basket full with self-healing attitudes, beliefs, and activities. Power animals can help guide us in this.

Power Animals and Power Animal Retrieval

As in Miriam's case, people often need help in obtaining the right power animal for their life circumstances. Quite often, by the time a person shows up at a Reiki shaman's door, the power animal a client needs is already circling around waiting to be allowed into the person's life in a vital way, having been unintentionally rejected time and again.

Subconsciously, people reject energetic beings and attachments all the time; it's an automatic response, like breathing. That's one of the ways of discernment that must often be rebuilt when people use heavy drugs in order to "see" shamanically. These "doors" of perception/attachment are natural protections, like antibodies or white blood cells. You don't think about them, but they are always there protecting your health. So, even positive, well-meaning power animals are often rejected unintentionally.

Once, I was doing a book signing on the Mississippi Gulf Coast and a woman called the bookstore, frantically asking if I was still there. Assured that I was, she said she was on her way. She arrived, bought a book, and left. But a few minutes later, she returned saying that she didn't know why, but Spirit just kept telling her to turn around and come back. She was confused and embarrassed, but I said it was alright, we'd see what was going on.

After finishing the book signing, we went into a side room, and I used what's called the trembling hands method of "seeing" energy in her energy body; that is, holding my shaking right hand a few inches away from her body to feel, or see, what's going on. I saw that she had a power animal and a couple of soul parts wanting to come home to her. I explained what I was doing, told her to relax, and guided the soul part and power animal to her heart chakra. She understood immediately what was going on, and was amazed.

It turned out, she had actually glimpsed the soul part as fleeting memories or perceptions but had rejected them, and the same with the power animal. Every time they would try to "seat" themselves in her, she would become frightened and start shivering or sneezing, which energetically rejected them. She was guided to the book signing—that was no "coincidence." I always tell my students: Trust in Spirit. Do as Spirit tells you. Our inherent wisdom always knows best.

Power animals come of their own accord, but we may not always recognize them. For example, one student said she didn't know what her power animal was, but after questioning, admitted that a hawk routinely would perch on a patio chair at her house peering in the window at her. Another woman said that she didn't know what her power animal was but, after questioning, admitted that crows followed her wherever she went and seemed to be speaking to her. A young man said he didn't know what his power animal was, but after questioning, admitted that he had always loved Siberian tigers, had a toy one as a stuffed animal as a baby, and still had a poster of one above his computer at home.

Here's a wonderful message from a client who was just recovering from serious illness and surgery:

> *I forgot to mention that I believe Bee has now entered into my life. A while back I rescued a Bee while I was out kayaking. Actually, I paddled right by him while he was floundering in the water. As soon as I passed him by something said, "Go back." I did, and after a few maneuvers found him again. I lifted him from the water on the end of my paddle and plopped him on my front hatch for the sun to dry him out. He seemed pretty clumsy and kept falling off into the water. I kept picking him up and putting him back on the kayak. I paddled toward shore and tried to place him on a mangrove branch. He kept falling off that, as well. I decided to paddle across the channel and place him on a concrete seawall by some grass and a tennis court. By this time I was quite attached to him! I lifted my paddle to the wall and tried to get him to walk off my paddle. He turned and walked toward me. Finally, he dropped off onto the walkway and started to walk toward the grass. As I paddled away, he turned and faced my direction as if to say thanks.*
>
> [He continued to find bees in need of help, like this one, until one morning he got up and found] . . . *what seemed to be a few bees covered*

in pollen darting from flower to flower quickly turned into hundreds and hundreds of bees all across my yard!! They were white from all the pollen!!. . .Now I love my yard!! It is so alive!

This person's experience is not an uncommon occurrence, where a chance but powerful encounter with an animal is followed by successively more striking encounters until the "connection" between the person and the animal totem is undeniable.

I wrote back to my client, telling him about Bee as a power animal:

The essential elements of bee as a power animal are these:

—Foremost, bees live in colonies and, while they are individuals, they also practice a mass-mind that gives them a unity of purpose and sense of belonging.

Each bee has individual tasks and each grows into ever-evolving duties. The bees are telling you that you can be an individual while also "tuning in" to support all around you and becoming one with others of whom you may not be aware. If at any time you feel lost, alone or frightened, close your eyes, become "one" with your bee power animal with the intent to return to the hive; and there, you will find a great source of solace, healing power, fortitude, and peace, shared among others.

Note: All is dark within the hive; bees chew bark and sap (propolis), which is itself a healing balm, to seal all cracks and fissures to maintain

*total darkness and a constant humidity
which they provide even in temperatu.
below freezing by bundling into a gro.
shivering together (creating heat and a viι
that literally causes them to hummmm or v._.ιate
warmth as one). They exist in the hive totally by
feel and second sight (inner knowing). And when
it's hot, they maintain a cooler temperature by
adjusting their wings to beat at the same
frequency—again to raise vibration rate, but this
time with a different intent; showing how united
meditation (prayer) can translate into real results.
The hive is the "womb" home most of us recognize
intuitively but fail to find in the "real" world. It is
real, though, and with bee as your power animal,
you can find it.*

*—Secondly, of course, bees make honey. That is,
they flit from flower to flower, enjoying the bounty
of the earth, while also deriving its sweetness. Bees
collect nectar and pollen; the nectar is processed by
the bees into its essential sugar and water into
honey, which is an alchemy of bee saliva. In other
words, the essence of the bee and her interaction
with her environment provides a transformation of
something fleeting (a flower) and beautiful into
something lasting (honey) and sustaining. It could
not happen without all the elements coming
together—flower, earth, sunshine, bee—to create a
new, unique beauty upon the earth. When you
become the bee, or tap into that energy, you are
sharing all the beauty of the earth and by your
mere presence you are transforming those gifts into*

a unique new gift that is not just beautiful but also sustaining to a larger population!

—Third, all but a few bees are female. The drones (males) mostly lounge around the hive doing nothing; their sole purpose is to vie with all the other wild drones in the area to mate with their sister, the queen, if they can, when she's ready. Then, their lives end. The importance here is that the beehive is raw female energy: female empowerment. For women, this can be life-changing; that focusing on pure female energy can provide structure and support for going forward. For men, to have the bee as a power animal can be equally powerful—allowing both sides of the personality to become balanced, to be able to see and feel in a complete way. Men in our society, normally, aren't encouraged to "get in touch" with their female side, and it's a source of imbalance in our male-dominated society. By focusing on the bee, and becoming one with the bee, a man can find tremendous healing power—reconnecting with source and foundational power that has been lost, forgotten, sublimated, or rejected in the past. In fact, I believe that the bee very well could be the power animal of this age—leading to a more co-equal empowerment and shift in paradigms.

As you can see, you have a wonderful new power animal!

People often come to have a power animal retrieved for them. Usually, it's just a case of giving permission from an outside source—the Reiki Shaman—to have a power animal. Not that permission is needed, but people often just seem to want an outside source to "confer" a power animal upon them; they cannot believe that a power of the universe would come of its own accord. But they do.

It also seems that clients for a particular power animal come in clusters. For example, a series of people with bee power animals may show up wanting a power animal retrieval. As noted in the above case, Bee is particularly beneficial for women seeking personal empowerment, seems to be connected to past lives in ancient Greece and Egypt, and is often associated with goddess energy. Bee shows up for women who feel as if they are not reaching their full potential and may come up not only as a power animal but a past-life remnant.

Past-life pieces are a bit hard to describe and are not often noted in shamanic literature—perhaps, because, unless you have a belief system that supports reincarnation, the soul pieces might be viewed as something else. Imagine the classic Super Mario computer games, where little icons such as a hammer or other objects empowered the character to perform magical feats. Well, a past-life piece could be seen like that. Essentially, they are boosters you give yourself while in the Bardo and deciding how you will live this life. For example, you may feel that your original life contract just isn't working out, or the choices you made weren't optimal. Then, perhaps, a new power animal will show up to help.

But, frequently, in the Bardo, you foresaw this potential life circumstance and saw also that you would need some outside boost or energy to help you find and achieve new goals or accomplishments. In this way, rather than journeying to retrieve a power animal that will help guide the person toward new life goals, there might be a "packet" of energy that can do the same thing: a gift from the client to the client from a previous lifetime.

For example, here is a journey for a person we'll call Tomi, who is a Reiki master, with Bee as a past-life piece:

Tomi Journey

Went to Bear Cave, met Bear, went to Sky Lodge.

Saw eagle, wolf, mouse power animals.

Saw ritual needs: Three pebbles, to ground, center, be present; bring containment/attraction power back.

Saw soul parts like paper dolls on a string stretching out, bring back.

Saw two past-life pieces: Lyre, golden bee.

Saw Reiki guides; needs to meditate on Reiki master symbol.

In this journey, we can see there's a lot there, although it's in note form. When I first started journeying for people, I thought I was missing a lot, so I tried using a tape recorder. When I listened to the tape, however, I found there were long pauses and then a jumble of words too fast to be recorded. So, I stopped that, but it helped me to see that the visions in the shamanic journey are in "all-time, no-time," so time doesn't mean anything. Journeys are perceived in consciousness as lasting plenty of time, and may even seem long and tedious, but from the outside they are bursts of information. There's too much to record, either in "real time" 3-D time recordings or written down by hand. So my method now is to journey, see what I can see, then write down everything I saw as soon as I return from the journey. If you choose to follow this method, you can flesh it out later, if you have to, or journey for the client again to see more when the actual work is performed.

For Tomi, I wrote an explanation of what was seen in this journey:

Interpretation

First off, there are some "normal" things that need to be done, such as returning some lost soul pieces (that are stretched out like paper dolls on a string), and there are three power animals that can help you at this time: eagle (to allow you to ascend to a higher perspective, and see the bigger picture), wolf (that can help protect you, while also connecting you to other, perhaps new, people) and mouse (which can help you focus on what is present and before you).

There are also two past-life pieces, energy or essence from former lifetimes that can help you at this time: a lyre, which is somehow connected to

music (and I'm thinking perhaps an origin in
Thrace), and a golden bee, that perhaps was some
type of ancient goddess sect (teaching to nurture
your "honey," value gathering and sweetness of
life, your feminine power, etc.).

Also, carry three pebbles with you. Carry them
with you at all times. Whenever you start to feel
lost, or sad, or disoriented, or unhappy, hold the
pebbles in your right hand and move them around
by squeezing them until you feel grounded and
centered, present in the moment. (It's actually a
way to bring your attention to the present, and
draw Earth energy up through you, to be released
as a grounding mechanism.)

Overall: It is important at this time for you to
bring your life back to center, to empower yourself,
and be totally in your own power. You have been
giving your power away. You have released a string
of soul parts off into infinity with your sadness,
worry, and unhappiness. It's time to reclaim your
"self." You cannot change your life by allowing
others to dictate your moods, moves, and overall
direction. You must reclaim your "self," your
actions, your thoughts, and your behaviors.

Then, you can decide what—if anything—you
want to do regarding your situation, whatever that
decision may be. It will be one of Power, and
acting, not reacting.

Finally, I saw the Reiki guides there, and the
Reiki Master symbol. I was told you should
meditate on the symbol. Remember that the figure
above is your highest self, and that is what leads

*you in this world, if you allow it to do so. It is
connected with your crown chakra. The middle
portion of the symbol is you in this world, the 3-D
world, on your Earth Walk. It is called "the fire
carrier." That is your heart beating, the fire,
connecting you with Creator. The bottom, sun and
moon, show you that you are literally walking
between the worlds; that the sun and moon are at
your feet, if you allow it. You are the center of your
destiny.*

*We want to reverse this "giving away" of your
power, and shedding soul pieces, so that you can
be centered, grounded, and empowered.*

After performing the work, I wrote a further
explanation of what was seen, felt, and done:

*The journey was very beautiful. Light and airy.
Felt like waves upon the shore.*

*Impressions: The lyre was very silver, brilliantly
shiny; it can help guide you: music, connect inside
with ancient stirrings, very old "knowings."*

*The bee was brilliantly golden, also connects to
ancient "knowings," but of a more physical and
practical nature. Expore what the bee symbolizes
and see where it takes you.*

*I also implanted the Reiki Master Symbol in
your crown chakra, to help guide you, and so you
can meditate on it better.*

*Regarding your power animals, look at their
qualities and see which ones you like and can use,
and ask them to help you with those qualities. Just*

look up the animals in books, or Google, and see what "resonates" with you. See which qualities you have that they share that you don't want, too.

At night, in your prayers, ask them to do things for you and you may be amazed at where they guide you or what they bring to you.

I did some extraction of spiritual intrusions from you; this will help you keep yourself energetically clear, as does doing regular Reiki treatment on yourself, or having it done to you.

I did a Reiki treatment on you, too, implanting the emotional symbols in your aura to help keep you clear.

The soul parts I saw were returned and they looked like a spiral going in, bringing in more lost soul parts. We want to keep that spiral going, so it's important that you do your homework, using your pebbles to stay present, meditating on the Reiki master symbol to keep you focused on who you are and open to be guided to where you want to be. Don't let others take away your power; keep yourself empowered. Also practice being in your body; really FEEL things; like water on your toes; making your body feel good, enjoying sensations. Allow yourself to feel pleasure in your body. The bee can help you in this; it is goddess energy; BE the goddess. You have permission to do this. It is important that you be in your body and feel all sensations without remorse, guilt or self-consciousness. You have given away your power for too long. It's time to reclaim it, own it; it is yours. It is up to you to choose what you do with it, no

> one else. *If this sounds selfish, it's not: It's SELF-*
> *ness—that is, honoring the self, not harming*
> *anyone, but making you a more powerful woman,*
> *so that you give more and to whomever truly needs*
> *it, as you deem it.*

Tomi's journey is one of several that came about the same time, over the course of a year, involving bee energy. In each case, though widely separated by geographical, racial, and cultural differences (literally across the globe from each other), the individuals shared the bond of needing healing empowerment as provided by the energy of the bee. Most came in the form of power animals, but others, as in Tomi's case, came in the form of past-life pieces. The process is basically the same, retrieving power animals or lost soul parts.

Soul Retrieval for Self and Others, and Returning Stolen Parts

Returning lost soul pieces is a shamanic practice whereby energetic pieces that have been lost, usually through trauma, are returned. We are always gathering and releasing energy in our lives, like respiration. But when trauma occurs, the amount of energy shed can be debilitating. Energy is shed so that the person does not feel all the pain.

For example, in an auto accident, the last thing one wants to experience or remember is the crash itself. So, the consciousness of the moment of impact is frequently shed. That's why people often can remember everything leading up to the crash and afterward, but not the crash itself. That energy (including the patterns of energy called consciousness and memory) is lost. But the body knows that pieces are missing and people (such as the woman at the book signing in the example above) know intuitively that important energetic pieces of themselves are missing or lost.

In most Native American cultures, warriors returning from war, for example, would not be allowed to mingle with the general population until they had been cleansed of all negative energy and lost soul pieces were returned. Otherwise, they were seen as not being whole—psychically wounded—and could contaminate the people with dis-ease, including negative or out-of-balance behaviors. (A number of American veterans organizations today are performing soul-retrieval practices, usually in conjunction with the Native American sweat lodge or *inipi* or *asi*. For more of these types of practices, see my book *Finding Sanctuary in Nature: Simple Ceremonies in the Native American Tradition for Healing Yourself and Others*).[5]

Sometimes, soul pieces are stolen. In ancient days, shamans would steal souls to frighten their enemies or weaken them. The story of the Iroquois (Haudenosaunee) lawgiver, the Peacemaker (Deganawidah), for example, tells how he brought order to the people by enlisting the aid of a powerful sorcerer named Tadodaho who was terrorizing and stealing the souls of the people in Dreamtime. Deganawidah tamed this behavior by combing the snakes from Tadodaho's hair—symbolically, giving him peace of mind. Presumably, the souls of the people were released and made calm.

Nowdays, most "stolen" soul pieces are usually inadvertent; a person pining for a lost love, for example, might give away soul essence to the object of desire; a harried young mother might look at her bouncing baby and wish she had some of that vitality. These are usually minor losses and gains that go on throughout one's life, much as a person sheds skin or heals from bumps and bruises. No one benefits from taking soul pieces; they belong to the person and cannot be used in any meaningful way by someone else. But sometimes a shaman must "steal back" soul pieces from someone who has taken some.

For example, a woman we shall call Germaine came to me because she was feeling sad, listless, and that something was "missing." I journeyed for her:

Went to Bear Cave.

Went to Sky Lodge.

Saw her power animal, a white dove, waiting for me. Could see her teacher in the background, but couldn't make out features. The bird took flight and I followed. Saw a man, kind of scary. Laughing, large man, with dark beard. He was bragging out loud. Loud, boisterous words. Couldn't make them out. Boasting, mean. Not sure who directed at. The bird led me behind him, and I saw that out of his pocket was something that looked like surgery gloves, plastic gloves. I could see the fingers of them peeping out of his back pocket, twisting to and fro.

I looked closer and the "fingers" of the gloves were little people—Germaine's face on each one, screaming, crying for help. I was horrified.

I asked the white dove to go around to the front of the man and beat her wings in his face, which she did. Bear and I swooped in and scooped the "gloves" out of the man's pocket. We zoomed away. In the distance, I could hear the man cursing. He wasn't cursing us, but the bird that was flapping wings in his face.

We came back to Sky Lodge and blew the soul pieces back to Germaine. . . .

In this case, Germaine was a nurse who had divorced. The man with the beard was her husband. Though they had been separated for several years, she felt that he had stolen her soul—and, in this case, she was right. He probably didn't consciously know what he was doing, but must have known on some level that he was hurting her, draining her. After this soul retrieval, she was able to start her life over with great energy and purpose. She certainly knew to guard herself energetically from then on.

We had to "trick" the soul parts back to the person to whom they belonged. But that's actually fairly rare. Since soul stealing isn't a common activity in our modern society, it's not often encountered. But it happens sometimes. For example, one woman who we shall call Gloria needed some help, and asked me to journey for her. This is what I saw:

Went to Bear Cave, met by eagle. Went to lower world.

Saw four men, two women squatting around a fire by a dry creek. They were dressed in skins and gnawing on bones. Eagle said they were a group (coven) of witches who regularly prey on people eating their psychic energy. They live in the Calif.-Ariz.-Mexico area. Saw that on the fire was big iron pot, with bones bubbling in it. The place was very sandy, a desert-like landscape, and there were dinosaur bones sticking out of the creek's sides. The witches didn't see me, as Eagle had me enfolded in his wings.

Eagle explained that Gloria was not specifically targeted by these people, but she came across their path and they had been feasting on her (stealing soul parts). They are marauders and opportunists who will feast on anyone.

There was still a tendril of connection, which Eagle guided me to cut. The witches weren't even aware of the loss. It was just one of many streaming/steaming from the big, black pot.

In this case, Gloria's soul pieces were easily returned, because the greedy, feasting *brujos* were too busy attacking and gobbling other people's life essence to notice. A short distance away, Eagle showed me the cast-off bones of what they had eaten: the actual soul parts, which we shook off, then returned. It wasn't the soul parts the brujos were after, but the act of eating that was important: attacking, stealing, and consuming. There was no benefit to their behavior except maintaining their element of power (as they saw it, anyway).

Soul parts frequently are stolen and then cast aside. Here's another journey regarding that for a man we shall call Victor:

Went to my crystal cave and met Bear.

We went into the underworld to look for a power animal. Was told he needed one. Saw several willing to come, but finally a crow came and it was the right one.

A man appeared. All I could see was his face, up close.

He had a very grizzled face, round with deep wrinkles, and his head was shaved.

He looked very grave, very serious.

I was told he is Victor's teacher.

Usually, teachers only show up in the upper world, but he was waiting for me. He wanted me to know how serious this soul retrieval is.

Very important.

We went to the upper world and Victor's teacher showed me the soul part that Victor needs; at first it looked like a cloak, but then I saw it was a large, white billowy shirt. Very bright.

His teacher told me that it had been stolen from him, but the one who stole it didn't want it and threw it away.

The shirt is important for it is his protection from negativity and darkness.

In this instance, retrieving the soul part was easy. I just blew it into my crystal, then along to Victor, who is my long-distance client, along with his retrieved power animal. There was much more to the journey, but this part of it is instructive, in that: (i) teachers only show up when it's important; and (ii) soul parts are often stolen and, almost as often, cast off again.

Sometimes, the teacher will show up during a soul retrieval, not only to show how important is the return of the lost soul part but also to give valuable clues as to the direction of the person's life status or choices. For example, a woman we shall call Justine came to me looking for guidance, and I found a regular smorgasbord of energetic work:

Went to Bear Cave, met by Wolf.

Went to lower world. Saw Raven/Crow. Raven/Crow sometimes difficult energy to address/harness: magic, power, holds good and evil at once; requires great strength and focus toward the light to keep in line with Higher Power, Higher Purpose. Can also play tricks; associated sometimes with the dark side.

Saw teacher, dressed as witchy witch but phasing in and out as something else—goddess of some kind?

Saw two more power animals needed at this time. . .

Went to upper world—Sky Lodge.

Saw four soul parts that looked like they were shed as a child—little girls in frilly dresses, connected by a tether or rope.

Saw needed extraction (clearing) of energy body. Dimly saw Reiki guides. Self-treatment would be good.

Told she needs to clear, let go—cut cords of attachments, release.

Should release all past-life soul parts to free herself up.

Ritual: Release captured soul parts.

In this case, Justine was the one who had captured soul parts in previous lifetimes and was carrying them around with her. I didn't journey into her past lives to see how she captured these parts, but it's possible she was a shaman or sorcerer back in time. The fact is, people often carry unnecessary psychic "baggage" with them that can be just as detrimental to health and happiness as soul loss. It acts as an anchor, or drag, weighing you down, so shifting and changing with life's natural twists and turns becomes hard.

There is an easy ritual to release past-life soul parts that are holding one down energetically. Go to a private place away from everyone, near water, and dig a small hole, and simply blow into it, with the intention of releasing past-life soul parts collected or stolen in former lifetimes. The feeling is one of energetically regurgitating into the hole, followed by a much lighter sensation, even lightheadedness. It's good to do this from time to time to stay "clear" energetically, since we are constantly picking up soul parts or psychic debris from others, and may also be picking them up in former lifetimes that are still being channeled to us. After all, time is a circle; "real" time is "all-time, no-time," and we are partially existing in other dimensions besides this one.

In Justine's journey, notice, too, that the missing soul parts were seen as "little girls in frilly dresses, connected by a tether or rope." What this tells me is that the soul pieces were lost during childhood and probably involved a loss of innocence of some kind, and since they were tied on a string, the behavior that caused them to be ejected was continued for a while.

Unlike some people who practice soul retrieval, I don't believe I need to know everything about the people who come to me for help. That's their business. Many of them were victims of abuse of some kind and wish to keep it to themselves. Also, I am not a psychologist, so I refer people to the appropriate professionals, rather than delving into problematic or pathological personal issues. Often, a client will say, "you hit the nail right on the head" and go on to explain the circumstances that caused the soul loss, but it's not necessary to know the particulars, in my opinion, in order to return a client's lost soul parts.

The fact that Justine's teacher showed up means that this was an important journey; but seeing the teacher phase in and out as a "witchy" type witch with black hat, and so on, was a bit disconcerting. When I told Justine about this, she laughed, and said she had been practicing wicca for several years, but was feeling that it was too confining for her and wanted to move on to something different. The fact that an image appeared of a goddess of some type could be a direction she might want to pursue, I told her.

The number of soul pieces found in a journey is immaterial; the ones that present themselves are the ones that are needed when the retrieval is done. But numbers and types can lead to understanding other issues. For example, sometimes we sabotage ourselves by not allowing ourselves to "go with the flow." The remedy for that is not to be light-hearted so much as to practice grounding on a regular basis. It sounds counterintuitive, but this was pointed out to me in a journey (with yet another bee as power animal) for a woman we shall call Bess, who had been collecting and shedding too many soul pieces over many lifetimes.

Went to Bear Cave. Met Bear.
Went to Sky Lodge.
Saw Bess. Needs extraction, especially right side, rear.

Saw Reiki guides all around.

Saw her Teacher. Looked like Mother Mary.

Saw Egyptian falcon—past-life piece.

Saw six (or so) soul pieces, fanned out, like in a bridge hand, connected with others.

Saw three power animals: bee, connected with past life, ancient divine feminine; wolf, protecting, showed so I could see her; owl, there for wisdom and journeying, if she desires

Was told she needs to release soul parts over many life times, and the ritual for release.

Was told she needs to ground, so completely, until she can only go up.

Was shown ritual: Needs to sit in mud, nice oozing mud; or if a beach is available, wet sand near water. Feel, really feel, connection with base chakra. Should have a crystal, hold hands together at the hara (just below navel), while sitting in the mud; allow release of unwanted energies through the crystal; while breathing in beautiful energy all around.

Do this once, and thereafter from time to time (without the mud, but remembering the mud, the feel of it—the water sucking away what's not needed; the energy acting as a two-way antennae to connect with higher frequencies, and discharge unwanted energies.

Drumming would be good for her. More Reiki.

Needs to connect with her divine feminine. Came through very strongly. Do hot/cold water exercises: sitting in bathtub, running hot water, then cold water on her feet, to bring attention back into body. Then, can imagine at any time this feeling, to ground wherever she may be; draw attention to being "in" her body, feeling all sensations.

In this case, we see that Bess is more connected with her "self" in multi-dimensions than in this one. As an aside, people who are subject to child abuse often "connect" with other dimensions during the abuse so they can "tune it out," including previous lifetimes and/or other universes. It's difficult sometimes to bring them back fully to the present, and so rituals to release souls that don't belong to them as well as fully grounding and centering in this world and body are necessary.

The process of allowing and releasing, and being open to new experiences, is central to the soul retrieval process. People who cling to pain or patterns of pain have difficulty experiencing the present moment, with all the joy, healing, and growth that's always available. While the aim of soul retrieval is restoring what is lost, the ultimate reward is allowing a richer, fuller, more rewarding life. That is done by releasing what holds one back while accepting that which pulls one forward.

Soul Parts Often Return On Their Own

Most people come to me for soul retrieval when they are in a type of anguish or anomie. The most common complaints are (i) feeling something is missing; (ii) aftereffects of drug or alcohol abuse; (iii) aftereffects of divorce or other loss; (iv) aftereffects of physical or mental abuse; and (v) aftereffects of physical/emotional trauma.

Often, the soul parts will return on their own. We have seen this with some of the case histories presented. The soul parts seen in the journey were once connected and people remain connected to all of their soul parts, even when they have been cast adrift since childhood. Since all soul parts have invisible cords connecting them, whenever a soul retrieval is performed, the process of shedding soul parts is reversed and pieces start returning on their own. So, whenever a client comes for soul retrieval, I always advise them to be open for additional pieces arriving of their own accord in the days, weeks, and months after a soul retrieval ceremony.

Once you have experienced soul retrieval and know how it feels, it's a lot easier for your soul parts to return simply by your intention that they do so, and allowing it. Soul part return is a natural process, often playing out beneath your consciousness. It may feel like a "remembering" of something vital you had forgotten. For example, perhaps you used to laugh a lot as a teenager and suddenly, you find yourself laughing again and remembering those old times. The feeling is frequently accompanied by such statements as "I haven't felt that in years. . . " Or "Where did *that* memory come from!?"

These remembrances of pieces of our soul are allowed into consciousness by a mental relaxation of barriers. I usually coach people to be open on a long car ride when thoughts are roaming (a "moving meditation"), or when in the bath tub and relaxing. Other ways of soul retrieval happen in Dreamtime, or consciously, when one "rattles in" their soul parts, using a rattle with the intent of recalling soul parts.[6]

There is a caveat here—one that I share with all my

students and clients. If the physical or psychological conditions that caused the soul part to leave still remain, then the soul parts won't stay. They will likely leave again. Also, soul retrieval is not a crisis intervention or healing technique for trauma as it is occurring. It is for returning to wholeness or completion within circumstances that can support that return. It is a tool for a healing journey that is already underway, not a substitute for the work of healing.

Great Distances Are Sometimes Involved

Sometimes, in order to retrieve a soul part, great distances must be traveled. For example, on rare occasions, I have had to journey all the way to what I call "the crack in the universe," the place from which we all came and to which we all return. When a person dies, the soul/consciousness passes through this portal to return "to the light," as most people envision it. If you pass through the portal, you are essentially envisioning your own death, and so your guides and power animals do not normally allow this to happen, except in death, or for a purpose such as teaching or healing.

This is the place that people often describe after a near-death experience. On the other side are various places that I've only been allowed to glimpse. (I can say that the feeling of such belonging, warmth, and serenity found on the other side makes it most difficult to come back! I told my wife Annette Waya that if I ever appear to have journeyed over there and am lingering, she should whisper "chocolate!" in my ear and I'll return. Gustatory pleasures, among other physical delights, are a strong attraction for returning souls.)

Sometimes, a shed soul part will make it all the way to the crack in the universe. Usually, it was shed during childhood and has made its way there, but it cannot pass through on its own. When a person dies, the soul parts that were shed over the course of a lifetime return with that person through the crack in the universe, unless stolen and stashed away somewhere, pulled along by the invisible strings or cords that connect them.

Here's a journey for a woman I shall call Susie, who had a soul part at the crack at the universe:

Went to Bear Cave and was met by Bear.

Went to the underworld and was met by a power animal for Susie. It flew all about so that I could see it clearly.

We went to the upper world and traveled a long way, to near the crack in the universe. I saw a soul part: a bright bird. I was told that it was lost innocence, lost long ago. It has a childlike quality—very innocent, fun-loving.

I was taken to another soul piece, which appeared like a dark pink rose. Someone had died, and this piece was associated with them. It was stolen from Susie or was held by the person who is deceased in some way, but could not be taken through the crack in the universe; so it is floating nearby.

I asked if there was anything more and was told no, not at this time.

I came back.

In this instance, I was told by the client that the person who had died was a close relative and she had, indeed, felt a tremendous loss with her passing. She never did feel quite "whole" again. She didn't elaborate on the lost childhood innocence, but acknowledged the accuracy of the statement. We performed a soul retrieval, which did help feelings of wholeness return.

In another instance of a soul part taken from a child, I journeyed to the crack in the universe only to find the deceased's arm sticking out through the portal with a soul piece. The deceased had stolen the soul essence of his child but could not pass in peace until it had been returned, and the daughter could not "let go" of the father after his death despite the passage of many years. The soul retrieval in this case liberated them both.

In other cases, it may be difficult to determine just what is returned, but it may have great significance for the client. For example, here is a journey for a man we shall call Ben:

Went to the Crystal Cave, met Bear, went to the underworld.
Immediately, met Ben's power animal.
It said it not only was it ready to join Ben but has been ready for quite some time.
We went to the upper world, kept going and going. . . all the way to the crack in the universe.
Was told that Benjamin lost this soul piece when he was 13.
Wasn't given particulars. But it has two aspects: this lifetime and a previous lifetime.
I saw it. It kept flickering between two images: a cross and a bird.

*When it's returned, it will return what was lost when he
was 13 and will return something that belongs to him from
a past life.*
Wasn't told anything else.
I asked if there was anything else and was told no.
Came back.
Aho.

I still don't know what this journey accomplished for
Benjamin, or the particulars of what was lost or
returned, but I do know that his life changed in many
positive ways thereafter. That's often the case with soul
retrieval.

Big Changes Are Often Wrought

Sometimes, upon completion of the ceremony, clients
report fantastic visions and incredible sensations;
others say they didn't particularly notice anything. But
in virtually every case, dramatic changes occur within
weeks or months—and even those changes are
sometimes unacknowledged. For example, one young
lady who felt lonely and unhappy came for soul
retrieval and said she didn't particularly feel anything
when it occurred. A year later, when I asked how she
was doing, she reported that "nothing" she could
determine had resulted from the soul retrieval.

But, after conversing for a few moments, it turned
out that within days she was offered a new job; found
an apartment and roommate much more to her liking;
met a man; they got married, and she was pregnant

with her first child! But, in her view, the soul retrieval had nothing to do with any of it!

The number of times people achieve dramatic changes in their lives after soul retrieval is so great—even if it's "only" a shift in attitude, belief, or way of viewing the world—that it's rare to find no change whatsoever. Usually by the time a client shows up looking for soul retrieval, consciously or unconsciously, the person is ready for the changes the procedure will help usher in.

More often than not, a person wanting soul retrieval has a lot more going on than a need for that one procedure, and that can and often does entail a great deal of work in the shamanic journey. That's why I routinely offer a "bundle" of services. If the person needs soul retrieval, I also include retrieving any power animals that may be needed at the time; extraction of any negative energies/entities; and a Reiki treatment to continue the healing process for a period afterward. I call it "an energetic tune-up and an oil change." Here's an example of a typical client/journey where a lot is going on in the person's life and much is required, for a woman I shall call June:

Went down to Bear Cave and met my power animal, Bear.

We went to the underworld to see if June needed a power animal. Was told that she did. Saw any number of them eager to be her power animal.

Was finally shown one, a water bird.

I put it in my crystal and headed toward the upper world.

As I was passing through the Christ Consciousness grid to the upper world, I was met by Ganesh, the Hindu god that helps to remove obstacles. Was told that he would act as a power animal for her, also. He appeared like a golden wisp but had the power of the earth—which is why he was on the earth side of the CC grid. So, I put this emanation of spirit— the power of Ganesh—in my crystal and proceeded to the place in the upper world where I do my work.

There, in this place, I looked down at June's energy body. What I saw was most strange.

There were angels all around her, everywhere. She is surrounded by angels and guides of various types, including Reiki guides. (Has she taken Reiki?? If not, she should; that is, they are there, should she choose to use them.)

I looked at her energy body with the question: what is holding her back?

And she appeared as a drum, like a medicine drum, but with golden streamers hanging off it.

I saw that the golden streamers are attachments to her place, where she is, how she is, and that is holding her back.

I was told that, yes, she did need a soul part. So Bear took me out farther into the upper world, and we found it.

It appeared as a letter, an envelope. I was told: "It is permission."

Permission to do what her heart tells her to do— something she had given up, or that had been forced from her many years ago.

So, I went back to the Sky Lodge, and I blew the soul part and the bird power animal and the Ganesh spirit to her. I saw them locate with her and anchor in her energy body, so she has them within and without.

I was told that the bird would range far and wide and would guide her to where she needs to go, if she will listen to his voice.

I was told that she can call on Ganesh to move obstacles from her path.

He is with her, as is the spirit bird.

They are now there to help her.

But, still, I looked at her energy body as it appeared to me, the drum with the streamer/attachments on it. There were about a dozen attachments and I thought maybe I ought to cut them and set her free. Bear said, no, that only she could undo the attachments, and it would be wrong of me to do it.

I was told: "Only she can beat her drum."

I looked around and on the other side of the drum, I found an obsidian knife. It was small, about 6 inches long, but very sharp. "See," Bear said, "she has the tool to cut herself free."

But I was told that she was afraid to use it. It would hurt someone—maybe someone of whom she is not consciously aware, although her inner wisdom knows it. With the permission (soul part), she can make the choice to let the attachments go, without cutting them; they will simply wither into nothing and detach.

While I puzzled over this, I was shown something else: it looked like an old suitcase, a tan, almost orange one. I couldn't tell if it were leather or Samsonite or what, but it was of middle size.

I was told that this suitcase can take her wherever she needs to go. She has it in her energy field. It is already there (although I don't know if it has manifested in material form).

I asked if I could see this house or place she was looking for, but was told that was not for me to see. She had to see it.

I did some Reiki work on her. There were a few spiritual

intrusions that were removed. I implanted a master symbol in her crown chakra to help her see with clarity, to help her see where Spirit leads, and some other work.

Then, that was all.

Aho.

As can be seen in June's journey, there were several moving pieces: the power animal, the soul retrieval, and other energies that were necessary for her spiritual healing, growth, and development. The journey also shows that she is in the midst of a wonderful acceleration of her life's walk, with so many guides, angels, and power animals clamoring to help her, and even past-life pieces like the luggage appearing before her. In June's case, too, her life changed dramatically after this soul retrieval was performed.

Sometimes, however, a client will appear for whom I can do little. He or she may be experiencing a terminal illness or be in the stages of decline before natural death.

Here is a journey performed for a young woman we shall call Adele:

Went to Bear Cave, met Bear.

Went to upper world to Sky Lodge.

Looked in on Adele.

She had lots of power animals/guides/angels around her—was in good hands.

Saw she had some matter needing extraction; extracted what didn't need to be there, around her sides and abdomen.

Saw she had lost five soul parts that were nearby – from surgery and also shed since I last saw her. Reimplanted them.

Did Reiki on her, on area of surgery and general energy body.

She has a power animal looking over her that I do not recognize. Looks like a dinosaur to me. But it obviously means something to her; she's very comfortable with it. Maybe it resembles a fantasy creature? Anyway, checked with Bear, and it is of no harm—not an angel but a power animal.

She has Reiki guides present from her attunement. Her mother can hasten healing by using the Reiki symbols they have been given, allowing Reiki guides to do their work.

Had a talk with Adele (subliminally). She is utterly disgusted with her life situation; the problem with her abdomen is, literally, that it "sticks in her craw." She is unable to swallow, so to speak, literally and figuratively, living the way she is. And now she's drugged, so she feels awful all the time.

I asked Bear to show me what was going on. I saw that the area that was repaired is not the only place in her abdomen that has problems. I saw a "leakage" of energy from the intestines, that they are not strong, and further issues could result. I also saw that her heart is very weak.

I put the long-distance symbol as a "bank" of healing energy over her and powered it up.

I sent Reiki to her mom, emotional healing.

That is all.

Aho.

Adele has been a client for many years and has had continuing health problems and repeated surgeries. Her body is just giving out. You always do what you can for people, but you cannot take personally whatever happens. That goes for the miracles, as well. The shaman is only a vessel for healing energies to pass through from the spirit world to this physical world. What the client does with these energies is up to their own agreements with life.

One of my clients was a woman in Japan whom the doctors said would die within weeks. We did a long-distance treatment, and I also gave her a long-distance Reiki attunement so that she could aid in her own healing. I attuned her family members as well, who were told to chant the names of the Reiki symbols while they were with her. In a matter of days, her illness went into remission, and she lived another two years—long enough to see a granddaughter born and to play with her.

A Native American woman called me and said that the doctors intended to amputate her foot because of her diabetes. Time was of the essence, so I visited her home and showed her how to do Reiki on herself. Then we collaborated in a ritual, so that she could sing to the Ancestors for their help and blessings. As the time of the surgery neared, her astonished doctor told her: "I don't know what you're doing, but whatever it is, keep it up!" And she kept her foot.

A Native American man I worked with was involved in a car accident. His mother called me in the middle of the night from the hospital. She said the x-rays showed he had a fractured pelvis and possible internal injuries, and they were going to perform surgery the next day. I did a journey for him, implanting Reiki symbols in his body, doing extraction and a Reiki treatment and also set up a Reiki grid—writing his name on a piece of paper with crystals pointing toward it from each of the four directions placed on a table top. The next day, the doctors did another x-ray and the "fractures" were miraculously gone! They said there must have been something wrong with the x-ray film emulsion showing "phantom" lines. Surgery was postponed, and he healed in record time.

In another case, a mother asked that I journey for her son, who was in a coma, to see if I could awaken him. I journeyed but could not rouse him. I could see what he was seeing. Of course, it meant little to me—mostly geometric lines and shapes—but it had great meaning for him. He was here for that purpose in this place and time and no amount of conversation or cajoling on my part would "wake" him up.

An elderly woman contacted me and wanted me to journey for her. There were many guides and angels around her who let me know that the woman was not long for the world. They showed me past-life pieces that would be beneficial for her to enjoy and offered areas that she might wish to visit in her thoughts and reveries—subjects she could look up in books and magazines that would stir up forgotten memories.

I wrote the woman and told her what I saw (without telling her I saw her imminent death). She surmised, I think, what I saw, or knew it was coming. We had a wonderful correspondence for a while, then one night I was awakened by deer spirits telling me she needed help. I sent them to her to aid her, give her comfort. A few weeks later, I received an e-mail from her family saying that she had died and they were putting her things in order and came across the e-mail exchange.

They thanked me for the comfort I gave in the woman's last months of life.

I journeyed for the parents of an unconscious child to see what I could see or if anything could be done. I had a wonderful conversation with the "child," and I use this in quotation marks, because this person had already developed enough in nonordinary reality that he was accessing universal intelligence beyond that of a mere child. He pointed out that his body was so damaged by disease it couldn't sustain him; he had to go. It was his parents' grief and attachment to him that was keeping him—barely—in the body; for his best and highest good, he really needed to be let go, so that he could pass on.

It was painful for me to relay that message, saying simply, as I do with all who are watching loved ones pass away: Be happy for the time you had together here. Be grateful you were able to share so much together. You will be together again, and will enjoy again all that you shared. Let go, with love.

Anyone doing this type of work must remember that Creator is in charge. We do what we can, when we can, and we do our best, but a person's health and well-being is always outside our control. Creator creates miracles; Creator is in charge of all of our destinies. Whether we see any event as good or ill is from our own very limited perspectives.

Shifting Realities and The Nature of Time

In the shamanic journey, we may often be called to travel great distances—to the crack in the universe for soul retrieval, for example—we aren't really traveling very "far" at all. We are where we are, and that is connected to everything, every moment.

As outlined in my earlier books, *Reiki Shamanism* and *Healing Plants & Animals at a Distance*, the energy body is viewed in varying ways by various cultures. The "universal" seven-chakra depiction is not universal, and was devised by the theosophical movement in the early 20th century. There are more utilitarian ancient Egyptian systems that I think more accurately describe the transmission of energy through the body, outlined by Drunvalo Melchizedek. Generally, the energy body can be described in sacred geometry as a star tetrahedron shape extending 27 feet (8 meters) in each direction in the 3-D world then continuing outward into other dimensions.

When a person journeys shamanically, awareness follows the lines of the star tetrahedron out into space and time. I believe Creator sees time and space as one: all-time, no-time—a circle. In the shamanic way of viewing the world, awareness follows lines of intention. So, it really doesn't matter if one journeys a long way or a short way because one is "here" all the time and "there" all the time. It is as the physicists now describe matter as "winking" in and out of existence and being in two places at the same time.

Your consciousness apprehends the "reality" around you wherever you are, if you allow it, even in other dimensions. As an analogy, consider the phenomena of persistence of vision, which allows us to enjoy movies. Perception occurs at 1/30th of a second, or about the length of time it takes to blink the eye, which is how strobe lights in a darkened room are perceived as "stopping," "slowing," or even "reversing" movement in a choppy way. The brain perceives the illuminated movements, then pieces the movements together as part of the system of encoding motion. But the periods of invisibility still remain; they just aren't "seen" or perceived as independent and equal units of time. The mind is tricked into seeing the jerky movements as continuous.

So it is with our consciousness and other dimensions. Our awareness is winking in and out in other dimensions, perceiving people, places, and things, but we may not be aware of these lines of potential connection along our energy bodies during the normal course of the day. Our realities are dreams of the Reiki Shaman, whether in shamanic journey, nightly dreaming, trance, daydream, or what we call waking reality, however we define it.

Our awareness is like a pea in a bushel basket—only a tiny fraction of all that makes up human consciousness (which we may call monkey-mind or ego or personality). It is constantly sampling the multiverse beneath our awareness, and helps explain how two people on opposite sides of the world can come up with the exact same idea, or create a breakthrough that changes the total consciousness of humankind, even before it is written about or displayed in the media. To a shaman, this connection with all places at once is located in the heart, which is a liquid oscillator going back and forth with its energies, inward/outward, reaching out to touch oneness with all things, then energetically returning, bringing life back into the body.

In Norse mythology, the Doppelganger is seen as a ghostly double performing a person's actions in advance, and, more broadly, of people seeing someone they know—or even themselves—in a crowded setting. It's because, in all-time, no-time, we literally are in many places at once in time and space.

This was illustrated in our home one day when Annette was teaching Reiki and the class was giving a woman a Reiki treatment while I was in my study writing this book. The woman was astonished to learn that I was not one of the people giving her a Reiki treatment, writing later: "I know you were typing your book, but you were also working on me and not just a little, I saw you distinctly just as I saw the others, with my physical eyes. I felt your hands and heard your voice. "

I wrote back to her:

I have no doubt that you saw what you saw!

We are each and all composed of many layers. Consider, when you are drumming or praying for someone, and someone else "pings," or comes to mind.

When this happens, I usually give a tendril of thought to acknowledge the person and continue with the matter at hand. For me, this is a form of prayer, to say "thank you" to the person for thinking of me, acknowledging that person's existence, giving gratitude. That is usually enough to have the energy of that person seem to fade while doing ceremony, drumming, praying, or other energy work (especially in the sweat lodge, where many, many people come to mind during the prayers).

But for the person who is doing the "pinging," the perspective could be quite different. From what I'm told, people have seen visions of 1) what was going on with me at the time, which could be a gathering of some kind, or images from the sweat lodge, or of me or others in ceremonial clothing, or others at the event, even past-life visions; 2) of me as my power animal, such as an eagle or bear; 3) conversations with me, or even, as you relate, healing work.

This especially happens during Dreamtime, during night-time dreaming, when people sometimes report long, detailed activities.

I have no recollection of these things, and am usually mildly surprised at them. But I have no doubt that the person saw what the person saw. For, we respond to the people around us in ways that often are "beneath the radar" of our consciousness.

Because something is not perceived by our ego mind does not mean that something didn't happen. Our ego mind/personality wants to "own" everything about us. But consider something as life-giving and essential as breathing. Unless we take conscious breathing up as a practice, we do it automatically. But we do it, whether we acknowledge the fact of breathing or not. So it is with our consciousness: We do many, many things subconsciously. If we are engaged routinely in the practice of energy medicine, then we are doing this also.

It is a good thing, too! I'm sure that you have given me, in return, many loving, healing thoughts, and Reiki energies without "thinking" about it. So, I thank you, for that, as well, though I may not be aware of it when it is happening or has happened.

The issues here are twofold: consciousness and persona, or intelligence located in the body.

People who are not aware of their night-time journeys may go about the universe in a fog—not knowing that their actions and behaviors are not real. They are sleepwalkers. All of us do this from time to time. Unless totally integrated in day/night consciousness, we are not lucid in reality/nonreality all the time. You may encounter hundreds of people in Dreamtime, even become familiar with them, and never meet them face to face, or know their names. This type of projection of consciousness, when brought into awareness, is called the shamanic journey, when using the drum. Or it may be called astral projection, lucid dreaming, or distant viewing when self-awareness is present, not using shamanic methods.

This mutability of consciousness is dependent on how we each define our reality and our abilities. If we define our lucid dreams as astral projection or as cases

viewing, then that is how we perceive and
em. But if we define this projection of
consciousness as entering nonordinary reality through
the shamanic journey, whether using the drum or
otherwise, then it becomes part of our body of
knowledge for practicing shamanism or Reiki
Shamanism.

The second aspect, persona, has to do not so much
with the location of consciousness outside the physical
body as within the body or self-identity.

As I explained in my book *Healing Plants and Animals
from a Distance*, which goes into this in greater detail,
our lives in this 3-D world can be seen as a medicine
wheel, or a circle divided by vertical and horizontal
lines. The divisions made by the lines are our rational
or ego minds attempt to make linear sense of the chaos
of the world. The circle is the world, or all that we
perceive. Most people perceive time as moving in one
direction around the medicine wheel; but the circle of
time moves both ways, clockwise and counter-
clockwise. Time moves both ways simultaneously;
Creator can perceive both.

The backward spiral is what is honored in *heyoka*, or
Sacred Clown traditions in Native America, honoring
the way Creator sees, the sacredness of time and being.
We stand at the center of the medicine wheel of the
world and create our own timelines through our
thoughts and actions. That is the power of each
moment. Each moment is a miracle, and in each
moment, in the blink of any eye, we can change
ourselves, our world.

At any time, with timelines, we can shift from one

persona to another, as well. Consider standing between two mirrors, one fixed and the other located on a revolving door. As you move the door, you would see any number of images in the other mirror of yourself reflecting again and again, ever smaller, seemingly into infinity. This is how we are in "reality." At any moment, we can choose to go this way, or that way, and each one of those images is in an alternate universe than the one being experienced, taking the "other" path. Each reflection of you has a slightly different perspective, a slightly different life, but each one is definitely you.

According to Hindu mythology, humans are Dew Drops on the Lotus Blossom. Each of the "dew drops" are our personalities or what we experience as ego or associate as ourselves. If you touch the dew drop so that it disappears into wetness, another will form to take its place. Both are made of the substance—life—that is in the air; and each dew drop is you: from the prime Giver, or lotus blossom, the manifestation of Creator.

In the Toltec way of ancient Mexico, each person arises from the cry of Eagle. How we each hear Eagle's cry is who we are: expressions of life in material form. There are myriad ways to hear (perceive, understand, translate) Eagle's call. In the ancient Mayan way (which closely resembled the ancient Cherokee cosmology), we each are the number that we vibrated in on, which can be allied or associated with an animal, totem, or immortal being.

In some systems of thought, at any given time, we have 12 other personalities we can draw from. There actually are innumerable ones, but these are the closest to who we are at any given moment. For example, if should happen to you in one timeline—say, ie, that you are killed in an accident—you over into a nearby timeline or reality. That is why, foi example, a person who has an accident of some kind, or is comatose for a while, often cannot remember key events or has a "faulty" memory about other issues. The timeline shifted.

The world is infinite, after all. How we perceive the world is as important as what we perceive in the world, for our timelines follow the "how" to the "what" to create our reality. Thus, time is mutable; an example of reality or how we may apprehend it.

Obligations and Suggestions in the Shamanic Journey

In practicing Reiki Shamanism for any period of time, you will find that there are as many complex journeys as there are simple ones. That is why I tell students to always take their power animal with them whenever they journey into nonordinary reality—or even "ordinary" reality, for that matter. Not only does your power animal protect you but it can explain the unexplainable, then guide you to what is useful, necessary, and safe.

While it's possible to journey without a power animal, why not benefit from one? Consider it like car insurance: If you just drive down the block every day, you may not need it; but if you go on trips and travel in traffic, sooner or later, you very well might. It doesn't make sense to not accept the help and guidance of these powers of the universe.

Ethically, it is vital that you always obtain pe before working with someone energetically.   ⌐y work is intimate—not physically but psychicall, and energetically. The energy worker is working with the most vital, essential, and personal aspects of a human being.

Remember, too, that in doing this work, we work *with* Western medical practitioners not *in opposition* to them. Some people come to me in hopes that I will tell them that they no longer need to take a medication or that they won't have to endure a medical procedure. I always tell them that they should do as their doctors tell them to do. I prefer the categorization of energy medicine modalities as Complementary/Integrative Medicine, rather than Alternative Medicine: what we do complements the Western medical model; it does not compete with or replace it.

By the time a person shows up needing major energy work, it's often too late to do the type of subtle energy work that can help turn things around. I always tell clients with advanced stages of health degeneration to go through with their Western medical treatments, then we'll work on healing. Miracles happen, but they are more often than not accompanied by a much greater shifts in awareness—a "healing" of mind and spirit helping the body along.

When clients come to me, I tell them to inform their doctors about what we are doing and assure them that it does not contradict any medical course of action. Medical schools today teach Complementary/ Integrative Medicine, and I've lectured to classes of medical students about it and practiced with patients in hospitals. There is no longer widespread stigma or fear about it, as when I was first starting out. Indeed, many nurses today practice Reiki and receive professional Continuing Education Units for taking Reiki courses. Nurses have made up a good portion of the students I've taught—and helped—over the years. Energy medicine in hospitals is burgeoning because of its effectiveness—and its complementary nature.

I always ask that any potential client fill out a confidential client information form that gives permission for energy work prior to doing anything, even if it's only to take a scouting journey to look and see what's going on in the person's life. I keep organized notes on everything I see. If a client calls me years later and says, "Remember what you did when you did that soul retrieval for me?" I can look it up and see. After performing hundreds of soul retrievals and other energy work, it's a useful tool.

People have criticized this approach, saying: "You can't be practicing Native spirit medicine with all this: keeping files and permission forms and charging for services." To which, I can only reply: Given what I know of Native ancestors, if they were doing this for the number of people that now require it, outside of the tribal setting, they would need a way to keep track.

As for charging for services: I will paraphrase Peter Catches Jr, a 38th generation traditional Lakota medicine man, who states that, in old times, people used to gift a horse just so that they could talk to a medicine man. Then they paid for services with blankets, because they were the most valuable items anybody owned. Now, people still try to pay him with blankets, and of course there are only so many blankets a person can use. He says that money is now what is needed and appreciated, and there is nothing inherently wrong with money. The object of exchange is not so important, as long as it is of value; it is the energy exchange that keeps things balanced. To take without giving sets up an energetic imbalance, which is not healthy for either party.

We live in a modern society, not the 18th century. We do what we can. We do it because we love it. We certainly don't do it for money because, as I teach in these books, anybody with training can work on themselves and others; we do it because we're called to do it by Spirit. Who can argue with Creator? If we are to carry on the old ways into the 21st century, we must be willing to adapt to the current conditions.[7] Either the old ways are used and shared in modern ways, or they are lost. By bringing old ways to new generations, the teachings of those who have gone before us live on.

Exercise 1: Going on The Shamanic Journey

The steps for shamanic journeying are very simple. Most people begin to learn how to journey by traveling to the lower world to meet their power animal. The power animal is a being—actually, a power of the universe—that accompanies you wherever you go. We are each born with one to attend to us. But power animals come and go, as our life circumstances shift and change. Usually, you have at least one, though some people— shamans particularly—can have whole menageries.

So, set your intention to go to the lower world.

To begin, drum, or have a friend drum a steady beat for you, approximately 70 beats per minute, or turn on a tape or CD of shamanic drumming (we sell a 30-minute CD on our website, www.blueskywaters.com, but they are available from many other sources on the Internet). Any type of drum is fine, although I find a single-sided hand drum is easy to hold for long periods.

A good first journey takes about 15 minutes. It may be useful to cover your eyes with a cloth to block out the light. Lie down, take a few deep breaths, and clear your mind. Imagine yourself in a cool, dark place, a waiting place, a good place to begin your journey. It could be a cave, or a place on a beach that you particularly enjoy. The main thing is that you want to have a hole nearby that you can go down into. Perhaps there is a tree with a bole in it in a park near your home. Some people even go down the kitchen drain!

Watch from this cool, dark place until your power animal appears. You will know it because it will appear friendly and open (no teeth, fangs, or menacing features) and will show itself from at least three different angles. You will know it is your power animal because it "feels" right. Ignore any fleeting images or animals that don't stop to engage you in a friendly manner as if it had all the time in the world (which, of course, it does!).

Once your power animal appears, allow it take you for a journey. Hop on its back, or let it guide you as you fly. After 15 minutes, have your friend drum you back, that is, double the tempo of the drum with the intention of energetically pulling you back into this reality. And you should wiggle your toes and stretch your fingers, allowing all your energy to come back into your body.

Once you have met your power animal, always remember not to journey without it! It is a Power of the Universe that will protect you from harm, no matter how great the potential threat. If nothing else, it will sling you into another universe to escape harm, allowing you to return safely. This goes for Dreamtime, too. In nighttime journeying, connect with your power animal; simply ask it to appear, and it will.

To keep it around, "feed" it with your good, positive energy: your thanks and gratitude. Put pictures of the animal or being, or one like it, perhaps cut from a magazine or printed out from the Internet, on your refrigerator, or desk, or altar, or carry one around in your purse or pocket. Also, read about the characteristics of the animal. Notice which qualities it possesses that you share, and which ones are qualities you desire, and ask the power animal to help you in these matters. You will be surprised what comes your way. Power animals are like stray cats: If you feed them, with heart-felt gratitude and appreciation, they tend to hang around.

Exercise 2: Being Here and There Simultaneously

Lie down on the floor, perhaps on a cushion or blanket and go on a shamanic journey. Ask your power animal to take you far away and then, for a moment, turn your attention to your body. You may be surprised to perceive the faraway surroundings and the hard surface of the floor on your back simultaneously. See if you can project your awareness so that you can see yourself. Your power animal may assist you by acting as a mirror, seeing yourself as yourself. This exercise can show you how you may appear to others in Dreamtime (perhaps as an animal or visage). It is also helpful in that it can be reassuring that you are always connected to your physical body. You may see a golden cord attached from you to your physical body, and your physical body in the shape of a star tetrahedron. However it appears to you will fit in with your conceptions of the universe, and often based on unexpressed or unconscious archetypes or cultural expectations.

From The Energy Notebook: How I "Found" Reiki

Miraculous healings have been reported by those using Reiki. I'm one of those who can attest to it: I am, literally, a walking example of the healing power of Reiki.

I came relatively late to the practice of Reiki, having studied shamanism for many years. In 1992, I had fallen out of a tree and shattered my left ankle. I was very fortunate that surgeons were able to put it back together. Afterward, I was in chronic pain. But, it's what set me on the healing path, so it was a blessing in disguise.

In 2000, I was at a shamanism workshop and I mentioned to my companion that my leg was hurting; a woman sitting behind us overheard and said that she was a Reiki master and, if I wanted, during the next 15-minute break, she would work on my leg. I said, "Sure."

When the break came, she held her hands over my leg. After a few minutes, the pain went away. I was utterly flabbergasted. I had lived with pain for years—it wasn't a question of "if" there was pain, but how much—and this woman, with essentially a wave of her hand, had caused it to go away. I said, "Ma'am, I don't know what you just did, but whatever it is, I need to learn how to do it!"

I had never heard of Reiki. As she explained it, the vibrational level of the stainless steel in my leg was not the same as the surrounding bone and tissue and needed to be equalized. I now understand, too, that the Reiki helped me to release repressed emotions/trauma, as well. It worked. And that set me on the path to become a Reiki Master/Teacher myself, so that I could share this with others. I've been doing it ever since. Now I walk, even run, normally, with no pain in my leg. I'm literally, a walking example of the healing power of Reiki.

Since then, I've given hundreds of Reiki treatments and attunements, sometimes with equally miraculous results—especially when combined with the shamanic journey.

Review

Journeys and their meaning:

- The shamanic journey is described and experienced in varying ways but essentially Reiki shamanism combines the shamanic journey with Reiki healing.

- Power animals come in diverse guises to help us in the long and short term.

- Soul pieces and past-life pieces can return on their own but often are rejected unless a shamanic practitioner recognizes and returns them.

- Always take your power animal with you for protection and to help negotiate what is "really real," or the "nonordinary reality" of all-time, no-time.

- Always obtain permission before working energetically upon anyone, respecting the people, places, and things around you.

Internet key words: *Bardo, reincarnation, soul retrieval, power animal.*

Internet references: *Super Mario Bros. "Power-up" abilities.*

Chapter Three

Practical Applications and Lessons

Creator sees all as One. It is we who struggle.
— PATHWAYS

Over the years, people have come to me to ask questions, take classes, and gain inspiration. Each book so far has been an offering of knowledge to a wider audience. But even though I have published about my experiences and ideas, I have found that the process of learning has not ceased. In fact, the accumulation of experience allows more knowledge to accrue, which, in turn, leads to questions, research, reflection, then refinements in my understanding and practical application of what I've learned.

For example, the ceremonial use of tobacco, in sacred manner, is often questioned by my students. I explain that the type of tobacco product marketed as cigarettes, cigars, and so on, bears little relation to the plant that is traditionally revered by indigenous peoples. Cigarette tobacco is grown using industrial agriculture methods, relying heavily on chemicals, then processed with additional chemicals to enhance its effects and addictive qualities.

The Power of tobacco as a sacred plant is that it helps ground the person; indigenous songs that accompany the sacred, ceremonial use of tobacco focus on the ability of the plant to transmute, growing from Mother Earth in its roots and leaves into smoke blown as a sacred breath shared with sky beings, carried up to the ear of Creator. It is the oneness of being with Earth Mother and Heavenly Father and the breath of all life. With tobacco ceremonies, the heart's yearnings are elevated to a higher state of being.

Although in Native tradition, it is considered a misuse of the sacred plant, those who are addicted to tobacco can be seen as needing the Power of it. The craving to be grounded, to be serene and calm in the face of adversity, and find solace in the earth are, to a degree, present in all smokers. Indeed, I was addicted to smoking for many years and weaned myself off it in part by singing tobacco songs, allowing the Power of the plant itself in its pure form to help me to overcome its accentuated addictive qualities.

It is because of this real and perceived aspect of tobacco that we acknowledge that people do not need to actually inhale the tobacco mixture's smoke when performing ceremonies using the sacred pipe, but offer the choice that one may "smoke" the pipe or may instead touch the stem upon each shoulder. The Power of the pipe (or *chanunpa* in Lakota) is undiminished, and the blessing is given and received either way.[1]

The same is true of using cleansing smoke to clear houses, land, and businesses. My first book, *Clearing: A Guide to Liberating Energies Trapped in Buildings and Lands*, included other clearing methods besides burning sage, such as cedar boughs, sprinkling water, Reiki energy, liquid smudge, or even programming small crystals. So, techniques and approaches are always shifting and changing, as experience demands. Questions I have been asked by students in the dozens of classes I have taught since the books came out—and from a growing international audience—have also led to an increase in the body of knowledge with which I work.

This section of practical applications and lessons is an outgrowth of successive classes, treatments of clients, and other questions over the years since the first book was written. Some of the knowledge is in previous books, but expanded to address or emphasize certain points.

Dealing With Malevolent Spirits

The most frequent question I am asked by students and others is, How do I deal with a malevolent spirit? Often, the question is asked with some urgency, with the person believing that he or she is possessed and seeking de-possession.[2]

Let me begin by saying that very few practitioners practice de-possession, and that's for a reason: few people are actually possessed. One must be in an extremely compromised mental capacity—essentially a zombie-like state—to be possessed. The mind has its own defenses, and people have guides, angels, and power animals who watch over them and prevent it. It does happen, but it's so rare that it's just not a practice for which there is much need. However, belief in possession has long been a part of the public imagination, fed by such popular films as *The Exorcist,* an American horror film released in 1973. Although such movies are purely entertainment, sometimes the fear generated leaves a lasting impression.

Here's an example of a client's complaint:

> *"I feel some form of entity (clearly a negative or evil entity) is attacking me, trying to take away my ability to function on a day-to-day level. I am in a spiritual battle with this thing that is trying to possess me, and hoping you can help me deal with this, or fight this."*

In years past, I would journey to look at the situation and offer suggestions. Let me say up front, that in all my years of journeying, I have not once run across a bona fide possession, although I'm certain they do, in rare occasions, exist. There are, however, many situations that may mimic or approximate the conditions that one might inaccurately believe is a possession. So, let me outline some usual scenarios.

Not all spirits are helpful, and just because a spirit is an unseen being does not confer any special divinity or status. Noncorporeal lifeforms are individuals and must be treated individually, as they reveal themselves.

For example, for the client who offered the above complaint, I journeyed and found that he indeed was being badgered, but it wasn't an attempted possession. Instead, it was the spirit of a medicine person he had known in a past life that was trying to get his attention, to warn him of impending danger or life challenges facing him. But, because the client had been taught by popular media to see the events and perceptions around him in a certain way, he could only understand these attempts to communicate as a frightening experience filled with danger.

In another case, the person feeling persecuted had been taking mind-altering drugs (*ayahuasca*) without adequate training in how to deal with possible aftereffects. The client had experienced marvelous shamanic journey experiences under the tutelage of two shamans in South America during a month-long vacation. A few months later, he called me for help. Malevolent spirits kept coming to him, repeatedly attacking him, disturbing his sleeping and waking hours.

In order to help him, I had to teach him the basics of shamanic journeying, ways of protecting himself, and discernment. Unfortunately, this lack of proper instruction and followup is an increasingly common occurrence for people taking *ayahuasa*. Although many of the shamanic vacations to South America offer onsite supervision by persons with experience in journeying with drugs, the client is often left with a false sense of mastery. Often they then continue to use the drugs here, without shamanic supervision or the contextual support of a community in which hallucinogenic or psychotropic drugs are used traditionally, and in sacred manner.

One reason we stress teaching drug-free shamanism is that all the "drugs" you need to vision shamanically are already in your body. The rhythm of the drum, the naturally occurring dream state, and learning to meditate and allow visions are all more than adequate for powerful, life-changing visioning, without possible dangerous and recurring side effects. In our fast-paced culture, short-cuts have a powerful allure, but we have found that short-cutting shamanism can have unwanted effects that take much time and work to dispel.

In this instance, I had the client re-form his energy body from the ground up, so that he could rebuild his confidence in what and how to see. The drug had effectively knocked down his ability to discern what he was seeing, and hence, he was seeing everything and being frightened/overwhelmed by what he saw. This fear acted as a lure for negative beings, which thrive on the low vibrations of fear, anger, and pain. The increase in those lower vibrations became a self-fulfilling cycle of attracting ever-more base entities. Because these lower entities are shape-shifters, able to assume awesome, gruesome, and terrifying aspects, he assumed that he was being assailed by incredible monsters all hours of the day and night. Because the drugs had taken away his "on/off" switch on what he chose to see or dismiss, he felt isolated, vulnerable, and depressed.

So, I put him on a pipe fast, or vision quest, with a circle of power around him.[3] By this, I mean that we put him outdoors for 24 hours with an energetic circle drawn around him, so that he was protected, with the instruction to constantly ground himself through his base chakra by visualizing extending a tendril deep within the earth. We had him develop his own grounding song that he could use to remind himself to ground, and aid him in doing so, allowing the good earth energies to flow through him and flush and repel any negative energies—much as a leaf on a tree, or tree itself, derives nourishment from the soil.

Protected, calm, grounded, and nourished by abundant Earth energy, from inside this circle of power, he could see the beings for what they were: insignificant nothings, like gnats or buzzing flies. He then could see clearly that these beings were only irritants—but in sufficient numbers and using his own unconscious co-operation, they had been able to deplete his energy. Armed with this knowledge, he was able to laugh at them when he went to sleep at night and dismiss them as mere pests during his waking hours. Starved of negative energy, the entities one by one faded away.

Employ Positive Energy, Reiki to Repel Negative Beings

It is important to note that most of the reports of possessions or attempted possessions or psychic attacks by negative entities are merely low-level beings that exist solely to feed off of negative energies. That is one reason why I choose to avoid watching horror movies. Why attract such beings? Watching these types or movies or television shows, or reading such material only lures the beings that feed on fear. They assume whatever shape accomplishes that purpose.

While some people may find a thrilling energy in imagining vampires—especially if something appearing to be one actually shows up!—it's not so much fun if the being won't go away and persistently saps your energy in daytime stalking and nighttime dreaming. After a while, you may assume that you are actually possessed. But that just admits defeat, allowing all psychic defenses to fail, leading to a spiral of depression. As with the client above, the victim must rebuild energetic barriers and confidence. A great way to do this is through Reiki.

Beings that thrive on negative energy cannot abide positive energy. Reiki is pure healing, positive energy. If you have any inkling of negative energy in your surroundings, place crystals around your house, such as windowsills and above doorways, outside around the walls or property line; or put orange peels on the edges of your property. Sit in the center of your house or property and drum, sing, chant, or meditate on the Reiki symbols, focusing the energy with the long-distance symbol above the house or property, and imagining the power-up symbol spread all around, with the emotional symbol sprinkled throughout. If you are practicing Reiki Shamanism and journeying to do this, place the symbols in this fashion. If you happen upon any negative energies, laugh at them! Send Reiki their way; they will scatter!

Semi-Possession Caused by Agreements (Energetic Cords)

Probably, the closest case to an actual possession I've run across involved a highly psychic individual, who essentially was tricked into "letting in" a malevolent being, and although not actually possessed, was maybe halfway there. If this person had not had a strong psychic constitution and had not, in fact, intuitively been aware of something amiss, it might have progressed into a possession over time.

The woman wrote to me saying she suspected she was possessed. So, I journeyed for her. This is what I saw:

Went to Bear Cave, met Bear. Went to Sky Lodge.

Saw (the woman) and entity.

She is not possessed but has a voluntary agreement: cords attached to entity.

Entity looked like big dark, grayish-black amorphous shape. Probably can shift into any appearance, but natural appearance is dark with sparkles in it, like eyes— intelligence.

Bear showed me how she can remove it: simply cut cords. Use sacred circle space and a knife. Ask guides to help. Do self-Reiki.

Came back.

Aho.

After talking with the woman, the full picture emerged, and it's one that can be seen as something of a cautionary tale for others.

Initially, the entity came through intuition, as a "voice" that answered questions or gave guidance. She came to rely on it. It was dark energy; it cannot escape that. But people often are "thrilled" by such beings, projecting personalities such as Lilith, Kali, others, so that they feel they are on the "edge," so to speak, enjoying the power of possibly forbidden fruit and getting away with it. Problem is, the noncorporeal beings can slowly, like a glacier, begin to take over, directing thoughts, bringing darkness and trouble into the world, which is what they thrive on: discord, drama, pain, anger, resentment, and so on.

The person infected with this type of entity thinks everything is normal, because it developed so gradually as a way of thinking. That person's responses to others incorporates its influence subtly at first, but over time it becomes a conditioned response, or habit, in "hearing" or heeding the intuitive voice. The discord becomes a normal way of living.

But others may not see this influence as benign, and wonder what has happened to their friend or loved one. (A warning sign is when a person says, "my guides tell me such and such" and the such and such causes others pain or merely confirms a risky, dangerous, or blindingly harmful egocentric behavior; the entity wants to increase its hold by confirming longings and hidden agendas, rather than revealing or promoting healthy, harmonious, and positive outcomes.)

Rather than perceiving the entity and the increasing reliance on it, the person affected may project onto others his or her own inner turmoil, blaming them or rejecting them for any pain, suffering, or discord. It's a cycle that usually results in increasing reliance on the entity and ever more discord until something happens to bring it into sharp relief and, hopefully, cause it to stop.

The person is not possessed; it's a voluntary association. The person has only attached to it energetically, as a symbiotic relationship, and the cords that bind them energetically must be cut. Only that person can cut the cords, or they are almost certain to grow back. By voluntarily cutting the cords, they cannot grow back unless given voluntary, conscious permission to do so (as in saying out loud "I want you back" or to allowing negativity to take over conscious thoughts and behaviors). Positive thoughts/energy repel the entity. So, to keep it away, once a cutting cords ceremony has been done, the person previously infected must simply think pleasant thoughts or say a mantra or turn on Reiki anytime its presence is felt. After a while, it will go away.

For this client, I outlined the cutting cords ceremony, as I do routinely for this type of "possession" or influence. It's also one of the energetic prescriptions or sacred formulas for cutting cords to lost loves, past relationships, or situations one wants to leave behind.

In the past, I would have journeyed and simply cut the cords. People usually feel a sense of relief afterward, whether they are aware of what's happening or not. I would tell them that I had cut the cords, and that was that. But what I found was that after a few months, weeks, maybe days, the client might start longing for the "old feeling" of being connected to whatever or whoever it was that was being released. That longing for the familiar discomfort of the relationship would cause the cords to grow back again.

So, rather than have to repeat the journey to cut the cords, I started having people do it themselves; that makes them responsible for their own behaviors and consequences, teaches them how to deal with it, and helps them regain personal power. The ritual is the same whether it's done once or a dozen times. (Various cutting-loose, clearing, protection, or letting-go ceremonies are explored more fully in my books, *Clearing*, and *Finding Sanctuary in Nature*.)[4]

You can do this in a couple of ways, whichever you are most comfortable with. One is to go out to a desolate spot (in woods, or somewhere you feel safe or will not be disturbed) and make a sacred circle. You can use cornmeal or tobacco and make the circle a little bit bigger than you are while sitting, standing, or lying on the ground. Within the circle, thank your guides, angels, and power animals for protecting you in the sacred circle and removing all cords and connections that you do not want or need.

Sit in the center of the circle and either pray, meditate, drum, or do Reiki on yourself, thanking the Reiki guides, angels, or power animals for healing the cords and insulating you from them, removing all unwanted influences from your life. Simply stating the intention out loud is enough, feeling it warmly in your heart. Then, you may if you wish, take a knife or stick and go around the outside of the circle "cutting" any cords. (Shamans will often use a "spirit knife" just for this purpose, and I have a couple of very beautiful and ornate ones that have been given to me as gifts, but it can be anything, even your bare hand. Simply bringing your intention of "spirit knife" to mind allows the object to be as you intend.)

The cords have already been removed by the sacred beings and your higher power, but this puts your intention forward into the future. Thank Creator and all sacred beings for keeping the cords from growing back.

Then, simply step out of the circle, erasing it with your foot, or in some way "breaking" it open. And walk away.

Whenever you feel that "old feeling" of wanting a connection, just let it go. Laugh at it. Thank Creator, guides, and angels that you no longer need it. As long as you keep your intention not to grow it back, it won't return.

If you ever feel the need to repeat the ceremony, it's the same—for this or any other connections you wish to dissolve.

Another way is to make a prayer stick and break, bury, burn, or throw it in a body of water. In this way of breaking unwanted connections, you take a stick of some kind, and wrap twine or yarn on it, tying knots in which you put intentions of what you are trying to be free of. You take your time, putting memories of how this connection (person, place, or thing) has helped and hurt, thanking it and your higher self for providing this avenue of growth, affirming that it is time for you to move on.

When you are through, give it to the elements of Fire, Water, Earth, or Air to take it away and transmute into power for good.

Employing Spirits for Protection

We may find ourselves singled out for attack by spirits for reasons we cannot comprehend. In cases like this, it is advisable to seek protection from our guides and power animals.

For example, one time I went on an extended "spirit quest," or period of traveling sometimes called a "walkabout," where the itinerary is decided by Spirit.

I spent some time at a sacred place in the desert of the American Southwest and was awakened one night in my tent by a spirit trying to strangle me to death. I clearly saw the spirit in Dreamtime: an Apache medicine man.

I journeyed to confer with my power animals on what should be the proper course of action and was told that I should carry a piece of blue cloth in my travels during this spirit quest and should mark the boundaries of my campsite with it. It was explained to me that this would indicate to the spirits of the land that I was on a spirit quest.

I just happened to have some blue cloth and tore it into pieces, tying strips onto the top of the tent and around the perimeter of the camp. The next night, in Dreamtime, the Apache spirit approached but did not touch me. My guides explained to him that I was on a journey of spirit and was not there to harm anyone and, in fact, was there to help by giving prayers.

Although the spirit did not become friendly in any way, it did leave me alone from then on. I kept the blue cloth on my tent for the duration of the trip.

This is, of course, not an instruction to use blue cloth for spiritual protection but to ask your guides for the correct course of action whenever facing an energetic challenge. It seems like an easy instruction, but even advanced students sometimes forget that their protectors are repositories of immense knowledge and can offer simple and effective solutions for complex problems.

In another example, many years ago, while performing soul retrieval, I found myself inadvertently interjected into a battle with brujos, or witches, who had been attacking the client. After employing various defensive measures against them, I grew weary of the conflict and ultimately journeyed to meet my teacher in the upper world who took us—me and the witches—to a higher level to resolve the conflict.

I say "higher level" because I cannot adequately describe what I saw in words; the level of nonordinary reality my teacher brought us to, frankly, was beyond my comprehension. I would say that my teacher, who lives in the upper world, guided my consciousness and that of the three witches to a place where he, essentially, addressed our individual higher powers (the level of soul that guides our destinies on Earth) and showed us that none of us was operating on the paths we had intended before we were born. If we chose to continue along that path, it would alter our existence in ways we had not foreseen. There was then an agreement made between us, and the witches were no longer an issue in my life.

Let me hasten to add that I do not believe such interventions—by angels; guides, including Reiki guides; teachers; and power animals—are in any way unusual but, instead, happen on a regular basis for all people. If you've ever been troubled by something deeply, then prayed on it before going to bed at night, and awakened the next morning feeling as if a burden has been lifted, and it comes to pass, it's the same type of help, only hidden from consciousness. Our "guardian angels," whatever we choose to call them, or however we choose to perceive them, are always with us.

The difference, for the shaman, is that many issues that the average person deals with subconsciously are consciously addressed and the mechanics energetically revealed. A layer of reality is exposed that has previously been—and for most people remains—hidden.

Reiki: Secret Weapon Against Harm

Those who practice Reiki have the greatest protection of all in guarding against harm: The mental/emotional symbol. Simply by drawing the symbol in the aura (above, below, all around), you are shielded from negativity. The symbol acts as a transmuting mirror for whatever is sent toward it, but reflecting back love, light, and healing.

To protect your home, you can program crystals with the mental/emotional symbol and place them on windowsills, over the doorway, around the outside perimeter, to deflect negativity. To program a crystal, hold it in your left hand; feeling the intention generated from your heart into your hand, draw the emotional symbol over the crystal, while chanting the name of the symbol. Then, simply place the crystal where you wish it to be. Every few weeks or so, reprogram the crystal either by picking it up and reprogramming it (clearing it first by holding it under tap water) From a distance, first invoke the long-distance symbol, then send the mental/emotional symbol to it with the intention of reprogramming the crystal.[5]

One may also journey shamanically to access—or meditate on—the Christ Consciousness Grid (also called the Plume of Quetzalcoatl) with the intent of facilitating it to bathe the property in clear white light, raising its vibrational level and repelling all harm. When performed in conjunction with Reiki, this helps the home or place become simply radiant and impervious to any outside negativity.

Being Present and Having Faith Are Vital in Dealing with Entities

As we discussed, not all noncorporeal beings are beneficial, and when dealing with energetic entities of unknown and possibly hostile intent, it's of utmost importance to remain present and with faith in the protection of the divine, in accordance with your spiritual belief system.

Once, for example, I was asked to energetically clear some land that, in the 1800s, had been part of a Louisiana plantation worked by hundreds of slaves. Included in the land was a mausoleum and cemetery that the landowner had complained had "ghosts" that weren't too friendly. (For more on clearing spaces, including "ghosts," extraterrestrials, and other unwanted visitors, see *Clearing: A Guide to Liberating Energies Trapped in Buildings and Lands*.)[6]

Even before I reached the mausoleum, I could definitely feel the character of the land change dramatically to one of dark foreboding, including the usual telltale signs of a subjective drop in temperature and distortion of ambient sounds. Armed with the knowledge that my spirit protectors would do their jobs, I went about my business: defining the sacred space, offering tobacco to the Powers for aid in clearing the land, using a rattle to break up unwanted energy, and burning white sage to purify the space.

As I was rattling the mausoleum, I could feel the presence of a negative entity. I could glimpse it skirting the shadows ahead of me, as I shook my rattle and swept the burning white sage above and all around me and toward the walls and ceiling, "sweeping" negative energy away to be dissipated. I caught sight of a casket in the corner, which enthralled me: an ancient black metal box with a rectangle of clear glass where the deceased's face would be. I had a sudden flash of someone suffocating in that box, buried alive. I found myself momentarily in fear. Then, suddenly, the entity appeared inches from my face as a tall, pale, dark-haired, banshee-like woman towering over me in full throes of a silent scream. I gasped, startled. At that moment, the burning sage I held before me exploded, sending sparks and flame everywhere, and with enough concussive power that it felt like I was punched in the nose.

That brought me back to the present. I started to laugh at myself. Here I was—the *great shaman* going to "clear" a "haunted" mausoleum getting "spooked" by a noncorporeal being!

I resumed my task with renewed enthusiasm, laughing and thanking Creator for the lesson, and the whole atmosphere of the place totally shifted. The entity fled, and the room became brighter, with a holy feel of raised vibration, and the prayers of believers returned to it. A statue of Mother Mary seemed to almost come alive. Outside, the sun seemed to shine again, and birds could be heard chirping. Harmony was restored.

When the client came to pick me up, and I hopped into the front seat of her car, she asked, concerned, "What happened to you?" I looked the rearview mirror and I had a bloody nose, my face was blackened with soot, and my eyebrows were singed. I laughed. "Oh, nothing," I said. "I just lost my concentration for a moment."

Staying "present" should always be the rule when doing ceremony of any kind. Sometimes, it's difficult, such as the example above, but you can employ little tricks of the trade that will do the same thing, such as saying a mantra over and over. One of my favorites is simply to survey the scene, repeating: "*Be* here now, be *here* now, be here *now*. . . " And vary the inflection: "*Be* here now, be *here* now, be here *now*," while focusing on various aspects of the environment around you. Another is to hum, or sing, from the heart. If you know sacred songs, sing them, or allow them to float through your consciousness. Or chant or tone the names of the Reiki symbols. All are good ways to ground in the present moment.

Christianity Blends Well With Reiki Shamanism

On the subject of positive influences, and the power of Reiki Shamanism, a question I often get asked is whether Reiki or shamanism conflicts with Christianity.

Absolutely not! Over the years, we have had hundreds of students of all faiths, including fundamental Christian beliefs. (One of my best students was the wife of a prominent, nationally known Christian minister who served as something of an unofficial Reiki ambassador to members of their flock and others.) Biblical passages can be found to both prohibit and support many activities, and that is true for Reiki, as well. Those who practice Reiki and shamanism can be seen as helping humankind by helping to heal the sick and offering compassionate care for the suffering.

Reiki is a healing modality that is non-denominational, as is shamanism, when practiced as a method for healing. Both are energy medicine approaches that teach techniques separate from religious or even spiritual belief systems, depending on the individual.

Normally, among family and friends, I refer to Reiki as a form of prayer, enlisting Creator and Reiki guides and the help of all my guides, angels, and power animals. I refer to shamanism as "visualized prayer." And I teach people how to journey by calling it "Riding the Drum in Prayer." Why not use all of our senses and our highest divine resources when praying for others?

Actions that bring spiritual and physical relief and are consistent with religious beliefs as taught by Jesus are part of the mainstay of modern churches today (and may be seen as "Gifts of the Spirit," as the Apostle Paul describes in I Corinthians 12; 4-12, 28-31), and these practices are no different.[7] Reiki, shamanism, and Reiki Shamanism can be a fulfilling spiritual practice in conjunction with any major religious belief. It is up to the individual to decide how it fits into his or her personal life.

On Running Across or Stumbling Upon Beings of Light

At the end of my previous book, *Reiki Shamanism*, I told the story of helping to heal a light being in *The Energy Notebook: The Light Being's Daughter*, where I described being very leery of participating in a healing ceremony with an unknown entity.

As it turned out, the experience was a beneficial one. Since that book was published, we have moved from the house where the being was encountered to a larger piece of land we can farm. The light being moved with us, and still appears from time to time, but it stays mostly away or hidden and only leaves hints of its presence. Indeed, it was the appearance of so many beings at our new home that led us to buy it. There were allies (wild spirits) in abundance—beneficial spirits of the land, sprites, and elementals—all of which welcomed us to the place.

As I explained in the early part of this book: If you allow yourself to apprehend reality, you will see light beings and other assorted noncorporeal entities as you encounter them. It is best to remain as neutral as possible around them during such encounters; and it's certain folly to summon beings of which you know nothing. There is a great deal of chatter in books and on the Internet about "summoning" various beings, and I've received my share of inquiries about how to do it. I usually say: Don't!

Summoning beings for the sheer thrill of it is like playing with dynamite. Even people with great knowledge can be ensnared by the lure of perceived power that such activities bring. Ultimately, though, it turns against the practitioner. The practice of willfully summoning beings is that of the sorcerer, and it is ego based; in contrast, the shaman or medicine person does the work of Creator by helping others unselfishly.

Consequently, those who go about their business seeing nonordinary reality, practicing discernment, and remaining neutral (especially routinely employing the energetic practices of grounding, centering, and shielding) may be privy to great wonders and meet all manner of positive and/or instructive noncorporeal beings.

For example, one day, on my morning run, I saw what appeared to be a fog hovering over the road ahead of me. I could see that a squirrel had been hit by a car and its body was lying in the roadway, but I could not make out the whitish vapor above it. "Too big for the squirrel's spirit," I thought.

As I approached, I apprehended that the amorphous shape was an ally or elemental spirit performing psychopomp (helping the squirrel's spirit to the afterlife) by orienting it toward the light, and I could make out the being's features. It was a tall, broad spirit that appeared to be wearing clothing from a previous century, though, of course, it was almost totally transparent.

The spirit did a double take as I trotted past. "You can see me," it said. A car blasted right through it just then, the driver oblivious to it and pulling way out of his lane to avoid me on the shoulder of the road. "Yep, I answered, gaining ground between us. "I've been watching you guide that squirrel's spirit."

The noncorporeal being followed along a few paces behind me, in awe. First off, it couldn't believe that I could see it; second, that I wasn't frightened; and third, that such a sight was apparently, for me, a somewhat routine occurrence. As I continued my run, we carried on a conversation for about two miles. Finally, after discussing the arrangements that I had with other allies, we came to an agreement of our own.

It told me its name—in fact, a he—and I had him repeat the name three times, to fix it in my mind, but without uttering the name out loud. He said that he had had interactions with humans before, and I could tell by the way he communicated, with antiquated speech patterns, that he had been around for centuries.

The conversation was very light and breezy. I asked about other allies and spirits of the land in the vicinity, and he answered without hesitation—also confirming some information I already had gathered or suspected. For example, he knew all about The Light Being's Daughter, and even offered the exact location where she enjoyed reposing (a pond I was acquainted with, about half a mile from our house). He also showed me (via insight, or shared vision) some of his past, though without much detail.

Apparently, he had been wandering around as a free spirit for a long while. I saw an elderly man who obviously had been his most recent human companion for many years, half a century or more, and had died probably in the 1960s, from what I could tell of the man's furnishings, TV set, etc., in the vision. The being said he came from "that way," pointing over the fields to the east and beyond, and presumably still resided. With that, we parted company in a friendly way.

After I returned home, I looked up the biblical reference to his name, which is a variant—though spelled and pronounced differently—of Jephthah. The Hebrew meaning of the name is "whom God sets free, or the breaker through," or "he opens."

The name derives from a character in the Bible's book of Judges, who was the son of Gilead, from Gilead. It is recounted that he had been held in bondage by the Ammonites and his half-brothers had driven him out to the wilderness, and "There gathered around him some worthless ["empty"] men, and they went out with him" (Judges 11:3). He was recruited by the leaders of Gilead to command a campaign against the Ammonites, and he had made a rash vow that if he won in the battle, he would sacrifice his daughter.

Remember: When dealing with beings that exist in whole or part with nonordinary reality, symbols are everything—that is their whole reality; it's only a piece of ours. If we fail to read symbols, we are only seeing part of the picture. What this being was telling me, by giving his name, was part of his essential character.

Reading between the lines, or translating the symbology, his "name" is a treasure trove of information.

First, of course, what this told me was that I was, in

fact, speaking with a being that some call djinns, jinns, or genies. The meaning, in this instance, is that God set him free from being purely an ethereal being. That means that he can take physical form or exist in the material world—he is a "breaker-through" the veils, so to speak, of walking between the worlds, and "he opens," or can grant wishes or bring or allow things back and forth.

The story of this son of Gilead (itself indicating that he is of ancient origin, before recorded time) says a great deal more. His fellow djinns drove him into the wilderness (human world), where he wandered with "worthless" or "empty" men (either humans who could not see him, or who wished to exploit him without virtue) until he was recruited for a great battle (presumably against evil, or for righteousness, since it was allied with the causes of freedom or escape from bondage). But to win this battle, he had to sacrifice something very dear to him (his daughter), perhaps his destiny.

Now, here the history gets murky. There is controversy over whether the historical figure of Jephthah actually sacrificed his daughter. Some interpret that his daughter was "given up to God," not as a burnt offering but given to God to live out her virginity "*for* God," much as nuns today, or in ancient times, often, among goddess religions, serve as attendants to sacred places or shrines. The passage could actually relate that he would give to God what presented to him first, or give a burnt offering if it were not God's which presented itself. Since human sacrifice was forbidden in Jewish law at the time, the story of this historical Jephthah has presented a puzzle to scholars. Did he break the law, or not?

What does this name-mystery mean? Does it mean that he would give great gifts to any humans who could apprehend him—what God presented to him first? Or would he give away the gifts he possesses to someone else if any human approached that was "not God's," or without virtue?

It can be presumed, given his name and its history, Jephthah's "battle" against bondage continues to this day in various ways. Quite possibly, in this revealed aspect, there is a "trick" here that is hidden; appearing one way, but in fact another, or variable given the circumstance. Not all is revealed by the name, just enough to beware, perhaps.

When speaking with this being (and apprehending shared vision), I did sense some sadness as a core quality, or something lost, which at the time I ascribed to the death of the elderly man who had been his human companion half a century before. But after researching the name, I saw there was much more. He definitely gave up something precious and vital to have his freedom in the world, and I suspect he will wander the earth for unfathomable time to come, feeling that void.

The reason I did not say his name out loud is because that summons the being. Evoking the name of an ally calls it into the present. Also, when one speaks the name of an ally, especially three times, "fixing" it into the 3-D world, one is bound to that being, just as the being is bound to the person evoking the name.

Throughout time, energetic tricksters have sought to

gain advantage over humans by having their names spoken out loud three times, to bind them or free them from some other obligation or bondage. So, a practitioner in these realms should be cognizant of what is spoken out loud. The precise spelling and phrasing he gave me as a variant of Jephthah is the intonation and energy of his particular vibrational signature.

The Ally in the Road is an example to be careful with beings you encounter that seem to have innate intelligence. Genii are known for manipulating people and getting what they want. One must be careful in making the acquaintance of noncorporeal beings, just as one wouldn't embrace just any human off the street.

Varieties of Light Beings: Allies

There are differences between allies in the wild, elementals, and powers such as goddesses and other beings that can be difficult to distinguish. In part, this is because various cultures call the same types of beings differing names. This is an issue that crops up from time to time with students and others, seeking information about beings they may have encountered or may be familiar with in their local areas.

In the case of the Ally in the Road, for example, I initially saw him as an ally—in my frame of reference, wild spirits of the land are called allies and may be enlisted to help or protect a shaman or medicine person from time to time, as long as there is an open agreement that the being has its own freedom and is not bound to the medicine person. This is for the well-being and protection of both the ally and the shaman. Allies naturally frequent areas away from humans, particularly wilderness areas, far from civilization, because the discordant noises or vibrations from industrial machinery, such as cars, factories, and heavy equipment, are often hurtful to them. On our farm, we have some that drift in and out because we live in a rural area surrounded by tens of thousands of acres of national forest land.

These wild spirits of the land are essentially elementals—beings with great potential power but limited in guiding intelligence. They can walk freely between the worlds, in and out of nonordinary reality, and are frequently seen as either moving limbs in a tree or bush on the ground or, sometimes, a blur in open space. They emit a hum that can be heard over great distance, and some aboriginal peoples call them by using "click sticks" or bullroarers. They are known to humans by making the sound "tok" that can be heard reverberating in the forest (and is very similar to and often confused with the alarm call made by a doe deer). Shamans have sought allies for aid in ceremonies and rituals for thousands of years, and they are known throughout the world by various names.

The reason they approach humans, especially humans who can apprehend their existence, is because they are attracted to the systems of energy humans employ to name and order the world. Human beings are the namers of things and in so doing, give order energetically to everything around them. Allies in the wild have no central energetic core, existing much as a whirlwind energetically: scattered, and with only limited cohesion.

In the past, sorcerers would "bind" allies to them, possessing them for their power, in order to do their bidding. But inevitably, the relationship would fail, since the ally would seek ever greater mimicry, including the qualities of both good and evil, and ultimately turn on the one binding it. (For every one "used," there must be a "user," and when the exploiter and exploited approach oneness, they cannot coexist; the one becomes the other, or they negate, or kill, each other.)

Many of the sentient "evil" beings one finds in the world are, in fact, allies that have won their release in one form or another from sorcerers. Allies in themselves are not evil—or good, for that matter; they simply "are," as forces of nature and a type of elemental that draws its power from the earth. (Djinns are elementals, as well, but with organized societies dating back before recorded time.)

So, if one finds an ally in the wild that wishes to be employed (gain coherence, or energy through being familiar, or coming when called, and doing one's bidding), it's imperative that the agreement be spelled out explicitly and out loud, with the central premise that both are free beings electing to cooperate for goodness and Creator's will and may dissolve the partnership at any time without rancor. This agreement gives the parameters of respect, tolerance and adherence to principles of a higher, positive force in the world that serves both equally.

I always tell my students to approach any sentient

noncorporeal being warily, but not with fear. This is especially true with allies, which will imprint fear upon themselves if they encounter it and, therefore, may behave irrationally.

Water Spirits

Water spirits are viewed in different ways by different cultures and are essentially elementals. Most are beneficial. But there are reports throughout history and various cultures of water spirits that will ensnare human beings, attempting to enslave them, or do bodily harm. If there is a malevolent spirit, it probably is that way because it is an ally that was "turned" or released with the death of its keeper, as mentioned earlier. Or it could be a malevolent spirit with a higher class of consciousness that has taken up residence at the water feature because it derives life-force energy from the water and its movement.

Depending on the type of being that it is, the water spirit's actions can range from mostly low-level frights (it can only harm through fear) to a high-level being that is ancient and deadly. Removing, banishing, or otherwise disabling a spirit is a skill in itself. There are very few people who do it, or can do it, because it requires certain skills (and promises regarding one's life) that most people aren't willing to give, or give up. Malevolent beings are best left alone. As outlined previously, a person can employ techniques to protect themselves from such beings, but fighting, disabling, or negating them head-on is a different type of work (exorcism).

Benevolent Beings: Slumbering Goddesses

In my book, *Clearing: A Guide to Liberating Energies Trapped in Buildings and Lands*, I enumerated types of energetic beings and their qualities. I have received a great deal of inquiries about them, especially slumbering goddesses, which I described along with ways to perceive and awaken them. Hopefully, *Clearing* is helping more and more people around the world to engage these powerful helpers.

In ancient days, they were everywhere. Every mountain, stream, wetland, sward, or prairie was home to one. Such entities benefited from the thoughts/prayers of gratitude and thanks by the indigenous peoples, being energized by ceremonies. As the peoples who venerated them died off, that type of energy ebbed, and many of these beings went into decline or slumbered.

They are still around in diminished capacity, however, and can be and are being revived. The fact that these goddess/light beings are in a growing number of people's consciousness adds to their vigor. Learning to journey shamanically can help people see them, or employing the methods in this book to apprehend reality can allow the blinders to fall away enough for even slumbering goddesses to be revealed.

Once a slumbering goddess is apprehended and appears to awaken, it is not necessary to provide tremendous amounts of energy to keep her active or to thrive. Goddesses are Earth beings and, along with other elementals, can acquire energy from the angles and shapes of land forms, from the power of water running across rocks, flowers opening, frost forming, leaves budding, and so on.

Keeping her in your thoughts and offering gratitude for her presence from time to time should be quite sufficient to keep her around and healthy. The reason goddesses slumber is because the people who fed them their energy to retain shape and cohesiveness (the namers of things) moved or died off, and they were forgotten. But, as with all divine beings, they reside in the universal mind as archetypes that are immortal, just not in the 3-D world.

Crossing Over:
Helping Lost Souls Through Psychopomp

One of the most frequent requests from both students and clients regards the crossing over of loved ones to the afterlife. The shaman is often called in to help others to the afterlife, when there is sudden trauma, such as from an auto accident, and also from disasters such as plane crashes, when souls may find it difficult to accept the reality of their death and are lost or disoriented.

I've frequently found myself doing psychopomp in Dreamtime, with sometimes dozens of souls needing guidance, only to find later in the news that a plane crash or other disaster had occurred. Similarly, on occasion, when journeying just to see what's up, my guides may take me to the scene of a disaster in some far corner of the world for psychopomp.

The procedure is actually quite simple: orient the

person "toward the light." Keep that phrase in mind. The soul may appear lost or dazed or asleep. It may appear as the man or woman curled up on the ground, or even floating in the air. If you are drumming, set your intention with the drumbeats to go "toward the light." If you are in Dreamtime, simply look up, and you will see the light, sometimes appearing as the sun in haze, sometimes seen as an electric "presence," more felt or known intuitively than seen. Take your hands and gently push the soul "toward the light." Within every living being is this "light" that it yearns to rejoin; in Cherokee, it is called the *nvwati*, or *osta nvwati*, the "good medicine."

This divine spark is a unified quality throughout the universe, and it seeks its own. *Ki*, life-force energy, that makes up the name Reiki (or guided life-force wisdom) is an expression of this spark of Creator that is within every "thing" and binds the universe. When you see flowing water, for example, the energy that you breathe in and feel is the release of naturally occurring *ki*. This *ki* feeds the elemental water spirits that live near it. The same principle occurs in fields of flowers or gardens, where the rush of energy when the sun rises, dew falls, winds blow gently to sway the flowers, release the *ki* from within the flora and fauna, feeding the elementals—the divas, sprites, and land beings.

So, when you nudge the lost soul with the intention that they go "toward the light," you are awakening the spark within that is the Creator's light, and orienting that person so he or she can continue on to the next step of life's journey. It takes very little energy or knowledge on your part; your power animal is there to assist and guide should the need occur. The soul will simply drift toward the Source that is Creator's light of its own accord, once oriented.

The Dying Process

The actual process of a natural death has been extensively documented in ancient Tibetan texts, translated into English in various editions of *The Tibetan Book of the Dead*.[8] The book of course, is not the ideal guideline for Westerners, as it deals with icons and archetypes of the Tibetan culture that may appear utterly foreign and even frightening to outsiders. Similarly, the ancient *Egyptian Book of the Dead* is so foreign that it seems to be simply a mythos—which, of course it is, but without the underlying power of belief.

However, the process in the Tibetan text is worth noting and understanding. *The Tibetan Book of the Dead*, actually, is not a "book," at all, but a chant that takes 72 hours or three days to complete; which is the amount of time it takes for the human to energetically leave the body and environs. The chant outlines scenarios of what one might see or encounter after leaving the body, what those experiences mean, and how to negotiate them.

The purpose of the chant is to assist the noncorporeal spirit to make the choices that lead to a state of bliss, rather than being reincarnated back to the earth plane with its toils and sorrows. In the absence of the right choices, it also advises on how to reincarnate, so as to avoid the most suffering. (It's noteworthy that when the chant became "set," or standard, during the approximate time period of the beginning of the European Middle Ages, it suggested avoiding the area now known as Europe, yet essentially said there was much to recommend North America. Although giving different names, it described fields of buffalo, vast forests of pine trees in what is now the northeastern United States, and suggested there was a higher level of human enlightenment among Native American societies.)

Most indigenous cultures that still practice traditional ways still perform some sort of "wake," or observance, lasting three or four days. It's not uncommon for people who are unaware of the time period to report "feeling" the spirit of the loved one still lingering and experiencing unusual events (such as lights or radios turning on and off, or other electrical disruptions) or perceptions (hearing music or seeing a butterfly or dragonfly or hummingbird that seemed to speak or communicate).

When I've been contacted to do psychopomp for a person who has recently died, I've had to explain that, if it's a natural death, the departed soul should be able to negotiate this step on its own without any outside help. Intervening in a routine crossing over can often upset people's ideas of death.

For example, I once was asked to journey for a woman who had died and, as is my practice to write down all that I see, I reported that I saw a young-looking, red-headed woman who was simply elated, looking willowy and attractive, and even appearing somewhat playful and mischievous. My client angrily wrote back that I apparently had seen the wrong person because her elderly mother was not willowy, or very happy, and certainly didn't have red hair.

Some time later, however, I received an e-mail from the client saying that she was mistaken. In clearing out her mother's belongings, she had found a photograph in which her mother was, in fact, appearing young, willowy, mischievously playful-looking and, in fact, had red hair. The woman said she had never known, or had forgotten, that her mother had anything but dark or gray hair and didn't know it was naturally red or had been so in her youth.

When the departed show up, they usually appear not as frail or elderly or sick, the state in which most people die, but as they appeared when they were happiest and felt the best. In this instance, the woman said, the photo she found was of her mother holding her as a baby, days after she had been born. It was her mother's happiest moment. And I think I "saw" the woman like this because it was what the deceased wanted her daughter to know: She was healthy, happy, elated after leaving this plane—corresponding to her happiest moment on Earth, when she gave birth to her beloved daughter.

It is important that when people lose loved ones that they allow the person who is dying to leave. Often, the grief of loved ones binds the spirits to their bodies, beyond any expectation of regaining a useful life. But because the person who is dying may not want to cause grief, or add to it, he or she will simply hang on, hovering above the body, watching the grief all around.

When a person is dying and there is no reasonable

expectation of recovery, energetically, the best thing loved ones can do is be grateful for the time they have spent with the person, reliving wonderful memories, and thanking the person. We can utter, "It's okay to go," or something similar. And, "We love you, and thank you for sharing your life with us." This affirmation of peace, allowing the person to leave for the next step in the journey of life, can add immeasurably to the dying process.

Dying is a part of life, as natural as birth. It is part of the process of living on this plane. We are partners with those who have come before and those who will come after. Each affects the other, as we all are in the great Hoop of Life, all connected.

Rites after death, to allow the spirit to leave, with the blessings of those left behind, serve dual purposes: they allow those left behind to exercise their grief, so that the healing process can begin, and also allow the spirit to be freed from any cords or attachments that would hold them to this plane.

Lives Often Extend Into Past Lives

The bonds among those on this plane often extend to previous lifetimes. Sometimes in the shamanic journey, a practitioner is shown past-life experiences to explain current issues or problems in this lifetime. Experiences can also be revealed by past life regression.[9] What is revealed can be quite pertinent to explaining our choices in life, or challenges encountered.

For example, one client for whom I did a past-life

regression was an expert snow skier before ever having been on skis. He discovered this talent on a ski trip he and other executives took, which was hosted by his boss. Unthinkingly, on the ski course, he went to the intermediate area and skied expertly. His boss exclaimed, "I thought you said you had never been skiing before!" He said he hadn't, but it "just felt right." His boss almost fired him for "lying" to him.

In past-life regression, it was revealed that this particular client had died in an auto accident in a northern European country only a few years before he was reincarnated. He had been a cross-country skier from childhood. In this life, his body "remembered" how to ski, though his mind was unaware of it.

In another instance, a client who asked for a past-life regression was shocked to learn she had been an antebellum, white slave-owner. In this lifetime, she was born in Mississippi as an impoverished black woman who had to work hard for everything she owned. We performed several past-life regressions, so that she could more fully experience these two diametrically opposed views of the world.

In a similar case, a woman and her daughter in this life had lived as master and slave in the antebellum South. Though mother and daughter had their usual spats, they seemed to have a particularly strong bond. (Mother-daughter, son-father, uncles, aunts, grand-fathers, etc., often return together to the earth plane; they are part of one's soul "pod," or souls who reincarnate with you again and again—perhaps your wife this time, your father next time, your child the next—and people may show up from several lifetimes back, being renewed in new circumstances, as you both learn your life lessons each time around.)

In each of these cases, past lives helped explain interests and life lessons, but they also can explain chronic dis-eases or disfigurements. For example, it was revealed through shamanic journey that one client had died in a barn fire. He was trying to save a horse that, blindly attempting to get free in the blaze, knocked him down and killed him with a hoof blow to the head. In this lifetime, the client had a cleft lip.

In another case, a client who had died during a mustard gas attack in World War I had suffered all this lifetime with asthma and chronic lung ailments and was seeking healing through Reiki Shamanism. In many cases, the application of Reiki healing coupled with the knowledge of what had occurred in a previous lifetime effected a cure. Clients often find that once they learn why a malady occurs, it begins to subside or symptoms decrease.

Past lives that are revealed in the shamanic journey often give valuable clues as to why a person has certain interests or recurring dreams. For example, one woman who was particularly drawn to ancient Egypt had suffered all of her life from intense fear of being in the dark or in enclosed spaces. It was revealed in shamanic journey that she had been an attendant to an ancient pharaoh and had been entombed alive with him to accompany him to the afterlife.

During shamanic journeys, several individuals have revealed past lives in which they lived in North, South, or Central American indigenous societies. This explained their lifelong interests in books, lore, or artifacts on those societies—often with uncanny or unexplained knowledge of sites or lore. There are instances where individuals would "see" themselves in Dreamtime either killing or being killed in battle, or falling in love, or living peaceably in a village by water and with a sense of complete contentment, or witnessing grand pageants or rites in ancient stone cities.

These images of past lives come into clearer focus during past-life regression or dreaming because we carry these memories with us all the time—just below the conscious level. Past-life regression is performed either through deep hypnosis or guided meditation. Both methods work, but guided meditations can be done by virtually anyone. They allow the conscious mind to wander hither and yon, becoming lulled enough so that hidden or regressed memories can rise to the surface.

Past-life memories often arise when relaxed, such as when soaking in the bathtub or a long drive, a form of "moving meditation," or during a session of therapeutic massage, when memories or trauma patterns lodged in the body are released.

People often experience these glimpses beyond the veil. They are often disregarded, with the exclamation, "Where did that come from!?"

Remembering the shaman's dictum that discernment is the first rule of shamanism, such impressions should never be discarded without examination. It could be that there are connections to current events, places, and personalities that transcend time and space, embracing both past—as well as future—lives.

Journeying into the Past, or Future

Remember that time is circular, not linear. A   ~y
into the past or into the future each has its own quality.
The difference is this: The past is "set," to the extent
that it comprises all that has led to the current
moment; the future is mutable, in that it consists of all
possible timelines from the current moment.

Whenever we journey, we are journeying into "all-
time, no-time" where past and future meet in the
present moment. Time as we know it is suspended—
carried "forward" only by our consciousness, or ability
to comprehend the passage of time. When we act, we
are carrying ourselves, our intentions, and our Dream
of the World, into the future. We are literally creating
our future at the same moment as we create our
present, based on our assumptions, beliefs, and
attachments to the past.

At any moment, we can change the future and, in
fact, we do so all the time without thinking about it.
For example, if I choose to ride to work rather than
drive, I have just changed the future. Both choices are
predicated on a common "thread" in the past—in this
case, whether I have a friend I can ride to work with or
whether I have a car available for my use.

At any moment, there are myriad potential timelines
that carry forward into the future, based on the
probabilities of action or behavior. So, the chances of
my driving to work or riding with a friend are high
probabilities; the chances that I jump into the sky and
fly like Superman to work are not high. That's because
the past time lines—myriad choices in the past—do not

favor it. Remember, Creator is infinite, the universe is infinite, and we have infinite choices, even though the probabilities of creating specific intentions may be low.

That's something to remember when you are journeying into time: both past and future are mutable. Wait a minute, you might say, past is mutable, too? Absolutely. We frequently change timelines without being conscious of it. That's the nature of miracles. They happen all the time without us being aware of them.

Suppose you are going about your life, making your usual choices, and one morning you wake up and just "know" something is different. You may not be able to pinpoint just what it is, but you are certain something fundamental has changed. You go about your business, and in the course of a few days the feeling fades. Everything goes back to normal.

If you are persistent, however, you can unearth clues that something did, in fact, change substantially. Sometimes, these events are called "realm shifting," where an object, such as a crystal will disappear, for hours, days, weeks, or years, then suddenly reappear in the exact place where it "ought" to have been. If you are observant, you might be able to piece together what disappeared, changed, or shifted.

For example, one day, driving to work, I "lost" 15 minutes. I don't know where they went. One minute, I was driving along the interstate; the next, I was looking at the clock and 15 minutes had elapsed, although I was still on the same stretch of road. I called home and reported this, and it just happened to come up that I had been wearing a certain shirt. I looked down. The shirt I was wearing was a different one. Something had shifted. (It was not the ordinary day-dreaming lapse of consciousness that can occur when driving.)

That is an example of a time shift, where time and space change. If you are observant, you can sometimes even observe words change on a page, if you are reading a book; especially if an historical event is listed. Say, a battle you know occurred December 16, 1542, and you find that now that battle is listed to have occurred December 16, 1545.

If you mention it to anyone, they are likely to say you are crazy, that every schoolchild knows the date of that famous battle. But, our time and space realm shifts all the time. It's why we have historical events for which there is no explanation, such as the Mayan and Teotihuacán civilizations disappearing. The realm shifted. There are innumerable Native American stories of clans and tribes that "danced" into another dimension, or out of this reality.

Those who danced away are often called "immortals," and they sometimes come to aid us. The Ghost Dance, the dance revival that was popularized by Wovoka in the 1870s (it actually was a Cherokee dance of the 1830s), was itself an attempt to recreate this shamanic dancing into another realm. (Dancing into another realm requires cutting all cords anchoring one to the consensus reality and, obviously, is not recommended.)

The nature of a miracle is that it goes forward and backward in time. Just as something is changed in the present, so it is changed through all that led up to it, as well as all the proceeds from that moment forward in is what is meant by the term Walking in allowing peace and harmony to be the guide ozho, or The Beauty Way in Navajo or Diné, ana . /uktv in Cherokee). Everything radiates out from a moment of truth. Peace and harmony is one with it. It is the perfect Stillpoint of all-time, no-time, which people call the Now. This truth is our reality in this 3D world, but it cannot be measured by scientists or comprehended. It is the essential element of the shamanic journey and, indeed, all modalities of energy medicine.

When you journey, you are entering "all-time, no-time," the Now, the Stillpoint, the time that exists when the pendulum has reached its farthest extension one way and is microseconds away from turning the other way, suspended in time and space. Your consciousness perceives the movement of the pendulum because that is time itself: the quality of movement that can be measured. In the realm of Creator, there are no distinctions; time can go either way in the circle.

To journey into time requires archetypes in our minds that help us negotiate the absence of time and space. Archetypal scenes and themes seem familiar because they are familiar; they *are* repeated again and again in all of the arts. (Books, TV, movies, visual arts, music, and so on.) You know them well, for even if a person were to exist without any outside culture to reflect these scenes back at you, they are in your dreams, remembered or not.

To journey into time is also to journey into our own deaths, because what we are seeing is the causation of us, and our end; it is the alpha and omega. The archetypes we see when we journey into time are at once familiar to us and a bit disconcerting. For example, you know you have journeyed to a place of your own death when you find yourself sitting in a featureless white room, with no discernable doors, walls, or windows. It seems timeless (because it is). It is a "waiting room." If you look around you, others may also appear to be there with you. Were you to continue, you might see a light at the end of a tunnel; the tunnel itself might appear as a small portal, behind which the brightness of the light is too intense to see what is within it or beyond it. That is the doorway to beyond that no one passes without leaving this world; it is from whence you came, and where you will go when your time on this plane is over.

If you find yourself in either one of these places, which are accessed through the upper world, simply thank your guides for allowing you to see it and ask to return to another reality; restate your intent, that you wish to go back in time.

Two scenarios closely allied with these places provide the ability to travel back into time. The first is the long, dark plain. You may have visited this place in Dreamtime. It is a walk that you might perform after you have left your body for the last time. It will appear as if you are trudging along a flat plain that is in shadow. It seems as if you walk and walk and walk and never get anywhere, just walking forever. You may see low, dark mountains off to either side, or far ahead, but they never get any closer. You just trudge on. If you look up, you will see the sun shrouded in low, dark clouds. The tendency is to look back down and continue to walk. If you do so, you will never get anywhere. You may even dream this again and again.

The secret is to continue to look up at that dark sun. If you continue to look at it, you will see that it will shift and change, essentially shifting and changing as do your moods or thoughts. That "sun" will eventually shift from symbol to symbol—it might appear as a giant eyeball, or as a pyramid, or any of a dozen other symbols that have hidden or enigmatic meanings, but the point is that you will slowly find yourself gravitating toward that light.

You will find, eventually, that you no longer are trudging along that vast, dark plane, and are instead freed of any restriction, able to go as you please. Just think it, and you are there. When you find yourself at that stage of freedom, then you may wish to go back into time. If you do that, you may find yourself able to envision any number of ways to do it, including another scenario, which may occur without encountering the long dark plane: Earth spinning in clouds.

If your intention in a journey is to travel back in time, it could be that you will have to go through these various scenarios to get there. They are associated with the critical elements of coming to or leaving Earth. Or you might be treated to a simple shortcut in the lower world to begin with: You may go down to the lower world in your journey and see Earth spinning on its axis amid a bank of clouds. The cloud layer, in fact, is the Christ Consciousness Grid, also called The Plume of *Quetzalcoatl*, but it appears as clouds. Your intention is to go back in time, so you fly around the earth the opposite way it is spinning. Your power animals will help you do this, and they will make sure you stop at the time and date that you require. To return, you fly around the opposite way.

It could be that you will not do any of these things, or will or will not see them with any conscious effort. But if your intention is to journey back in time, or forward along your current timelines, you may encounter such scenarios. It is good to be prepared for them.

When you journey into past lives, and forward and backward into time, you will find that it becomes easier and easier, and your own past-life experiences will more easily be accessed. Once the door is opened, they start to come unbidden with greater frequency.

As you become more adept at apprehending the reality that's at hand, both obvious and covert, on the outside and the inside, it becomes ever more obvious that reality has far more shades and colors than can be imagined. Learning to play the cords of perception beyond the single span of five senses provides an orchestra of meaning that often cannot be explained. It is there that the symbols we see become more "real" than the reality we can measure, and the understanding we derive becomes richer still.

That is what is meant by becoming, as a Reiki Shaman, a man or woman of knowledge. And that standpoint of discernment is where Power resides. Can you "see" what Eagle calls? Can you "hear" the heart of Earth? What presents itself when you open your eyes and heart to what is before you? This is knowledge—

your knowledge—that is reflected in the world around you, in all dimensions.

Keep a log. Experiment, practice, use your shamanic skills and Reiki in your daily life, in Dreamtime, and in the shamanic journey. It is through these inner and outer journeys that we develop as Children of Earth and Sky.

Exercise 1: Defining Your Purpose in the Moment

Allow words to emerge in a meditative state. For example, what does the word "Creator" mean to you? To your heart? To your mind? You might say: Creator is the Power of the Universe. So, as the Power of the Universe, what does that mean specifically to you? You might say, Creator as an infinite being, with all Power, knows no pain or sorrow; or knows all pain and sorrow, and so on

This is called an Ascension Test, because at any moment we can ascend to our highest state of being—indeed, we are there all the time—but accessing it in any current frame of mind can be something of a test.

The goal of each meditation is to find a few words that express Truth, Beauty, and High Vibration, so that you may enjoy it again and again.

Try it. Play with the words, as they are symbols for ideas. Over time, you will be able to "connect" with that state of mind (higher vibration) to create new ones and lift you to a higher state.

Write them down, share them with others.

Chapter Three: Practical Applications and Lessons

Exercise 2: Intuitive Life Lessons

In everyone's life, the same issues come up again and again, or so it seems. How often in your life have you asked, "Why does this always happen to me?" Similar events happen again and again until we successfully negotiate that life lesson, as part of the Medicine Wheel of our lives. We'll keep going around and around, hitting that wall or barrier until we learn to deal with it.

To help learn your limitations, it can be useful to heal with numbers.

First write the numbers 1 to 10 on a page. Then, beside each number, write a quotation or some lesson that you have found to be true. The quotations or lessons can come from anywhere, as long as they "ring true" and seem to apply to issues you come up against again and again

For example, you might write: "To See the Harmony, Be the Harmony." Or, "Discord Arises Only When the Ego is Involved." Or, "When the Path is Dim, Seek the Illumined Path Within."

Keep this list handy in your notebook or in a top desk drawer. When you feel uncertain, life seems "out of whack," count from one to 10 and see which number seems to "resonate." Look up this number on your list and see which quotation applies. You may be surprised at how relevant it is.

171

From The Energy Notebook:
Reiki Guides Seen Shamanically

For those who practice Reiki but not shamanism, or vice versa, I can say that it's quite an experience to work with the Reiki guides in nonordinary reality.

The first time I journeyed after receiving a Reiki attunement, I saw the Reiki guides as a gigantic pillar of purple, like a purple totem pole, with the faces of the guides stacked one atop the other seemingly stretching into eternity.

As I was marveling at this, my own Reiki guide appeared in a swirl of purple.

He took me into the purple pillar and I "became" Reiki energy.

It was as if I were looking through the eyes of a fly—a thousand facets.

If I moved forward, I could see through each facet, focus through one at a time, where hands were being placed on people for Reiki healing.

I "was" the energy. I couldn't see the whole body being worked on, but only the part where the hands were placed, and my purple healing energy was flowing into that body.

If I pulled back, I could see the thousand facets again, as I floated in the purple pillar. Wherever people were laying on hands for healing, using the Reiki energy anywhere on the globe, I was a part of it.

It was very beautiful and timeless; I could have stayed there forever. But human time is much more limited than that of the spiritual beings and I had to return.

Since then, I've acquired several Reiki guides who often accompany me in my journeys and assist in healing in nonordinary reality. They also appear in nightly dreaming, and transport me to people and places needing healing work.

From The Energy Notebook:
Attachment to Old Ideas Affects Behavior

In my books, I've said again and again: Everything is energy, patterns of energy. Additionally, I've emphasized to my students that the first rule of shamanism is discernment. That is, to be cognizant of where your energy is going.

Energy losses can be due to staying in Dreamtime too much, and not being present in the 3-D world enough; or recognizing that you are siphoning off consciousness to nebulous and faraway worlds (not grounding and centering). Or, it can be something as simple as clinging to old ideas.

Old ideas that are no longer relevant are like the hoarded things in a closet: they keep us bound to old ways that no longer have meaning.

An example is with our monthly newsletter. I started it in 2000 as a way to keep in touch with students, drum circle members, and others who were practicing energy medicine. I would type out activities that we were involved in, as well as local news, what friends were doing, and listing workshops near and far.

The first newsletter was a few pages long and sent to about 50 people. It quickly grew. By the time a year had passed, there were nearly 1,000 subscribers and the newsletter was 10 pages long. This was weekly, mind you! Written off the top of my head, just whatever I felt was important for people to know or that I thought might interest them. It was a blog before there were blogs.

After a couple of years, I cut back to once a month

because my energy medicine clientele and ceremonial duties had grown enormously. By 2004, including listservs, publications that reprinted it, as well as individuals, there were about 6,000 people receiving the newsletter monthly—in 28 countries around the globe.

I remarried in 2005. After about a year, Annette asked me why the newsletter was so long—usually seven pages. An e-mail newsletter, she pointed out, should be shorter, or people won't read it. Also, by then, it was getting almost impossible to send the newsletter out without glitches and returns, as SPAM filters were weeding out most mass e-mail mailings. Annette took over the newsletter's composition, and we switched to a professional e-mailing service.

What we found out was a reality check. The service kept metrics, and what I found was that only about one-quarter of the people who subscribed to the newsletter even opened it; most just deleted it. Of those who read it, most only spent less than a minute on it. All this time I had been imagining every single subscriber carefully reading each word!

I had to do some rethinking. Why did I write such long newsletters? It was partly because a devoted reader told me how much she enjoyed reading each one in its entirety. She then printed and bound them. So I produced the newsletter with a volume number and individual issue number so people could keep them in sequence and bind them into volumes if they wanted. That was my "reality," the perception that ordered my thoughts and behavior.

Once we shifted to a professional service with a statistics page, we found out that such was not the case. The truth was that people wanted only a short newsletter with many separate items and a few hyperlinks to "click" on for greater depth.

My wife also pointed out that our livelihood partly depended on selling books and other items on the web pages, and that the newsletter should also function as advertising.

As new forms of communication/social media became available, such as Facebook, Twitter, blogs, ebooks, we have adapted.

I could very well have continued writing my seven- to ten-page newsletters, with very few people actually reading them, or I could have quit writing them for all the time and effort they required—simply because the reality in my head did not reflect the actual world.

Whether it's a newsletter, or any other activity, it is imperative that we live in the present: practicing discernment and determining the truth and validity of our perception of the world. We must routinely question the suppositions for our behavior and worldviews, so that we are certain that what guides our behavior matches the current reality and is adapted to what goes on around us. And we must be able to cut the cords energetically to old ideas, behaviors, even localities that no longer serve to advance us and allow us to live in a healthy, viable manner.

This is the way of the world. Our Dream of the World is constantly shifting and changing; sometimes we have to play catchup!

Review

Practical applications:

- Possession is very rare. These are usually low-level entities that through shape-shifting appear to be frightening so they might consume negative energy. They may be dispelled by Reiki.

- Ceremonies of cutting cords are useful in letting go of painful circumstances or attachments. When coupled with release ceremonies and grounding, centering and shielding, they can allow greater nimbleness in facing life's situations.

- Reiki, shamanism, and Reiki Shamanism are compatible with major religions, as they are nondenominational practices.

- Becoming familiar with archetypes can aid in journeying backward and forward into time.

- Everything is related and has power in the Now, which is eternal and connects all things.

- Practice shamanic journeying and expanding your world.

- Allow yourself to be an agent of healing, practicing Reiki in the shamanic journey and in Dreamtime.

- Consistently thank your power animals, guides, and the Creator.

Internet key words: *power animals, totems, nonordinary reality, Akashic Field, Christ Consciousness Grid, Plume of Quetzalcoatl*

Notes

Preface

1. We teach classes in how to journey (www.blueskywaters.com). The Foundation for Shamanic Studies also teaches beginners how to journey and offers advanced training in its workshops. For more information, contact the Foundation for Shamanic Studies, P.O. Box 1939, Mill Valley, CA 94942. Phone: 415-380-8282. Website: www.shamanism.org. Also, see Alberto Villoldo's Four Winds Society at www.thefourwinds.org.

Introduction

1. PathFinder's PathWays are popular meditations/ observations by the author that have been reprinted in newspapers, magazines, and websites all over the world. They are designed to allow a broadening of understanding and perspective that at the same time raises the rate of one's vibration. Since they were begun as "Ascension Tests" in 2002, they have been included in each of the author's monthly newsletters, *Keeping In Touch*, which has subscribers across the United States and 28 foreign countries and on his website, Healing The Earth/Ourselves, www.blueskywaters.com.

Chapter One

1. "Laboratory spectroscopy of hot water near 2microns and sunspot spectroscopy in the H-band region" by Keith Tereszchuk, Peter F. Bernath, Nikolai F. Zobov, Sergey V. Shirin, Oleg L. Polyansky, Noam I. Libeskind, Jonathan Tennyson, and Lloyd Wallace. In *The*

Astrophysical Journal. September 20, 2002. The American Astronomical Society, 577:496-500.

2 "Mysterious new 'dark flow' discovered in space" by Clara Moskowitz, SPACE.com, September 23, 2008, referring to an article: "Top 10 strangest things in space. Nearby evidence for dark energy: does the universe have an edge?" from the Oct. 20 issue of the journal *Astrophysical Journal Letters.*

3. Fractals can also be seen as a method used in ceremonial healing practice; see the author's *Healing Plants and Animals from a Distance: Curative Principles and Applications,* Findhorn Press, Findhorn, Scotland, 2007.

4. "Physicist discovers how to teleport energy," *Technology Review.* Wednesday, February 3, 2010. Massachusetts Institute of Technology.

5. Masahiro Hotta at Tohoku University in Japan has expanded this concept to transport energy itself, allowing the ability to inject quantum energy at one point in the universe and then exploit quantum energy fluctuations to extract it from another point.

6. For more, see *Finding Sanctuary in Nature: Simple Ceremonies in the Native American Tradition for Healing Yourself and Others,* Findhorn Press, Findhorn, Scotland, 2007.

7. See Nagualism; books of Carlos Castaneda, also the author's *Healing Plants & Animals From a Distance,* Note 3, Chapter 1.

8. For more on how Reiki is a form of shamanism, see the author's *Reiki Shamanism: A Guide to Out-of-Body Healing,* Findhorn Press, Findhorn, Scotland, 2008.

9. This unified field theory and the fractals associated with this "Scaling Law" are integral to the theory of a

"Holofractographic Universe" developed by Nassim Haramein and Elizabeth A. Rauscher.

10. For more, see Dr. Goswami's Web page:
www.amitgoswami.org

11 See Tereszchuk, et al., Note 1.

12. "Phys ed: Does lucky underwear improve athletic performance?" by Gretchen Reynolds, *The New York Times*, July 28, 2010.

13. "Keep your fingers crossed! How superstition improves performance" by Lysann Damisch, Barbara Stoberock, and Thomas Mussweiler, *Psychological Science: A Journal of the Association For Psychological Science*, May 28, 2010.

14. "Coat of Power" by Maria Czaplicka, abridged extract of *Shamanism in Siberia, Sacred Hoop*, Issue 68, 2010.

15. *The New Science of Giambattista Vico: Unabridged Translation of the Third Edition* (1744) with the *Addition of Practice of the New Science* (Cornell Paperbacks), Ithica, NY: Cornell University Press, 1984.

16. Quieting the metate is what the vision quest or pipe fast is all about. For more on this aspect of learning to see reality, see *Finding Sanctuary in Nature and Healing Plants and Animals from a Distance*, Note 4, Preface.

17. For more on synchronicity and the shadow self in earlier books, see the author's *Finding Sanctuary in Nature,* Note 6, and *Healing Plants and Animals From a Distance* Note 3.

Chapter Two

1. The mechanics of the shamanic journey are more fully explained in the author's previous books *Healing Plants and Animals from a Distance*, Note 3, Chapter 1. and *Reiki Shamanism*, Note 8, Chapter 1.

2. See the author's *Healing Plants and Animals from a Distance*, Note 3, Chapter 1.

3. The author and the Foundation for Shamanic Studies teach core shamanism, Note 1, Preface.

4. For more on Blue Eagle liquid smudge, see the author's website: www.blueskywaters.com

5. *Finding Sanctuary in Nature*, Note 6, Chapter 1.

6. For more on rattling in soul parts and other healing rituals, see *Finding Sanctuary in Nature*, Note 6, Chapter 1.

7. For more on charging for services, see the author's website, www.blueskywaters.com under articles: "Ugista ti–The 'pay' of medicine men."

Chapter Three

1. For more on pipe ceremonies, pipe fasts, and other ceremonies, see the author's book *Finding Sanctuary in Nature*, Note 6, Chapter 1.

2. Alicia Luengas Gates, a former Franciscan nun who lived with the Yaqui tribe in Mexico, teaches depossession with the Foundation for Shamanic Studies. For more information, see the FSS website, Note 1, Preface.

3. For more on pipe fasts, see the author's book, *Finding Sanctuary in Nature*, Note 6, Chapter 1; for more on drawing energetic circles, see the author's *Clearing: A Guide to Liberating Energies Trapped in Buildings and Lands*, Findhorn Press, Findhorn Scotland, 2006.

4. See the author's previous works, *Clearing*, Note 3; *Finding Sanctuary in Nature, Note 6, Chapter 1; Healing Plants & Animals from a Distance*, Note 3 Chapter 1; *Reiki Shamanism*, Note 8, Chapter 1.

5. For more on crystals and their uses, see *Reiki Shamanism*,

Note 8, Chapter 1; also for more on the healing properties of stones, see Annette Waya's website, Bear Walks with Wolf Studio:

www.blueskywaters.com/animaltotemnecklaces.htm.

6. See the author's previous works.

7. For more on Reiki and Christianity, see Reiki For Christians: www.christianreiki.org. Also, in recent years, there has arisen a teaching by Karen Furr called Christ-Centered Shamanism, with the motto: "Bridging the teachings of Jesus and Shamanism as a way of life, we gain new insight into what it means to be 'Light of the World.' See www.spiritdrum.org.

8. For more on this, see *The Tibetan Book of Living and Dying* by Sogyal Rinpoche (Harper, 1994) and *The Tibetan Book of the Dead* by Padma Sambhava and Robert A. Thurman (Bantam, 1994).

9. For my clients, I use an amalgam of past life regression meditations, but recommend *Regression Through The Mirrors Of Time* by Brian L. Weiss, M.D., (Hay House, 2008).

Glossary

allies. Wild spirits of the land that can aid in healing and protecting natural habitats.

all-time, no-time. The present, accessed at its deepest level.

angels. Emissaries of light of divine origin that accompany humans through life and are available for assistance and inspiration.

animus. The spark of life.

antahkarana. Ancient healing symbol, thousands of years old, that can be used for local and long-distance healing.

apprehend. In the shamanic way of viewing, to take hold of, arrest, or seize, as perception in an act of understanding, in the moment, without judgment, or projection of consciousness.

archetypes. Attributes existing in potential form that can be brought into manifestation; original models after which other similar things are patterned.

ascension. Transcending to a higher level of consciousness; the next step in human and planetary evolution.

assemblage points. Areas in the energy body that "connect" us to what we perceive as reality, both with our senses and beyond our senses, to ground us into a reality we can perceive and understand.

aura. Emanations of the energy body, often seen as colors that show moods, thoughts, or potentials; energetic fields surrounding the physical body, including physical, etheric, emotional, mental, astral, etheric template, celestial, and causal.

authentic self. Who you really are, not who you think you are, or have been told you are by outside sources.

black swan theory. Outlined by Nassim Nicholas Taleb in his 2007 book The Black Swan, Random House (2007), the theory explains how unexpected events can have a huge impact on history, and how again and again our perception of what is possible conflicts in dramatic ways with unforeseen—but in hindsight—probable events.

brujo. Witch, masculine form, Spanish (feminine *bruja*; masculine plural *brujos*; feminine plural *brujas*).

centering. Locating the core of consciousness in the body; drawing magnetic energy from the earth and electrical energy from the sun to operate with balanced awareness.

chakra. Sanskrit for circle or wheel; In Indian Hindu thinking, the energetic centers in the core of the body linked together by a central psychic energy channel.

Christ consciousness grid (also called the Plume of Quetzalcoatl). An energy layer surrounding the earth that signifies the earth's highest potential and that was supposedly established by higher beings, often referred to as ascended beings, to help humanity through the current "shift of the ages."

cleansing. Transmuting energy to a higher, more positive form by raising its vibrational rate.

clearing. Dissipating (transmuting) negative energy. Clearing spaces usually also cleanses them since the act of clearing raises the vibrational rate.

co-creating. Operating as a partner with the Creator to boost positive energy.

crowdsourcing. A method of producing content or solutions from a willing audience. Inner crowdsourcing is a method of connecting with ancestors and/or significant noncorporeal beings.

ego. The survival mechanism, which is part of the personality. See personality.

energy. Subtle power manifested through life force, frequency, or cohesion.

energy body. A body that exists beyond the physical plane; in humans, such a body extends 27 feet in each direction, and thereafter continues into other dimensions. See aura.

fast. See vision quest.

fractal. A geometric pattern repeated at ever smaller scales to produce shapes and surfaces that cannot be represented by classical geometry but can recreate irregular patterns and structures in nature.

flow of creation. The movement or stasis of energy in a given moment.

God vs. Creator. God is one, all; the Creator is the active aspect of God as expressed in the will of creation.

goddesses. Land spirits of the highest order, usually associated with a place or characteristic; also, humans who have transcended but chosen to remain on Earth in spirit form as a means of service.

grounding. Connecting with the earth energetically to ensure that consciousness is not operating from other dimensions or overly affected by other energetic forces.

guides. Spirit helpers, soul brothers or sisters from former or future lifetimes, or spiritual masters who have assumed a supportive role for a particular soul's evolution.

healing. Bringing to harmony and balance, wholeness.

heart song, or power song. A song that expresses the unique, positive energies, traits, and intents of an individual, usually discovered through fasting and prayer.

higher power. God as expressed through one's highest nature.

kachinas. Supernatural beings revered by the Hopi and appearing as messengers from the spirit world; spirit beings; objects that may be crafted to represent the spirit body of beings.

lela wakan. Lakota term meaning "very sacred."

ley lines. Grids that crisscross the earth and hold potential electromagnetic energy, many of which were identified by ancient peoples, who built sacred sites over them.

life-force energy. Energy that is all around us in nature and that is emitted by the earth.

light body. Energetic body; the quality of energy around a person, as opposed to their physical body. See MerKaBa.

matter. Patterns of energy we perceive as having substance.

medicine. The inherent power within all things.

medicine wheel. A Native American system of prayer, meditation, and discovery, recognizing that life follows a circle. The wheel's directions and their significance, concepts from which all things are said to derive, include east (newness, discovery), south (youth, growth, healing), west (introspection, setting sun, light within), north (wisdom, elders, ancestors), center (soul, spirit), above (Heavenly Father), and below (Earth Mother).

meridians. Lines along the body where energy is channeled; often used in acupuncture and other energy medicine to effect healing.

MerKaBa. In sacred geometry, a star tetrahedron; an energetic framework that forms a blueprint for spirit to attach and from which, in plants and animals, DNA creates a physical expression; a geometric form that includes the light body; a pattern of energy shared by animals, plants, stones, and all objects, including those that are man-made.

mind of God. Expansion of human thought to higher consciousness as far as is conceivable.

morphogenic field. A universal field encoding the basic pattern of an object. From the Greek morphe, which means form, and genesis, which denotes coming into being. Noncorporeal beings manifest in three-dimensional reality through morphogenic resonance.

nagual. In Toltec shamanism, what is really real (nonordinary reality), as opposed to what we think is real according to our consensus reality; everything that can be. See tonal.

native peoples. Indigenous cultures practicing traditional nature-based ways.

nonordinary reality. Reality as seen when everyday constraints and predispositions are eliminated through trance or other methods.

personality. All that we adhere to, or believe, that makes us who we think we are. See ego.

pipe fast. See vision quest.

portal. A vortex through which objects and entities can pass from one dimension of reality to another while realm shifting.

power animal. An animal that offers guidance and protection; a totem.

power song, or heart song. A song that expresses the unique, positive energies, traits, and intents of an individual, usually discovered through fasting and prayer.

power spot. A place where all energies of a structure or tract of land are focused.

prana. Universal life-force energy.

prayer stick. A stick, either ornate or plain, that has been consecrated through prayer; wrapped with cloth, ribbon, or yarn; and most often, planted in the ground to carry a prayer.

random rat. The routine practice by scientists to throw out information that does not fall within predictable norms, perceived as an anomaly.

rattling. Shaking a rattle to break up energy or bring in energy.

realm shifting. The movement of objects between dimensions; while some objects, such as quartz crystals, do this routinely because of their energetic composition, others will disappear and reappear only when near a portal.

Reiki. A Japanese form of energy medicine involving sacred symbols and guides; use of the hands to channel healing energy.

sacred circle. All beings in our lives—past, present, and future—who are connected to us; consecrated circle for ceremony.

self-talk. The inner dialogue inside our minds; the "what ifs," "buts," judgments, and fears that prevent us from being who we really are.

shaman. Siberian word meaning "one who sees in the dark"; a person who uses earth energy, guides, and power animals for insight; a medicine man or woman.

shielding. Creating, through intent, a protective energy layer around you to deflect external negative energy.

shift of the ages. Powerful changes in energy patterns now occurring on Earth as a prelude to Earth transformations and humanity's eventual development of higher consciousness.

skan. Lakota word, meaning "power of the wind"; a sacred force of movement; that which existed before God; life-force energy; the principle that manifests prayers from prayer flags.

smudging. Burning a plant such as sage, cedar, or sweetgrass to purify the energy of an area.

soul. The essential life force, or essence, of a being that is eternal from lifetime to lifetime.

soul retrieval. The act of retrieving soul parts, or essence, lost through trauma or stolen by another individual.

space. Any defined area, including the objects within it.

spiral of ascension. Spiral of life that offers a changing perspective as new lessons are encountered and old ones repeated, until the lessons are finally learned.

spirit. The essential quality of a being as an expression of soul; noncorporeal aspect of a person aligned their with soul purpose.

spirit quest. Following only what spirit dictates, usually over the course of days.

star beings. Beings from the stars whom cultures around the globe and throughout time have claimed influenced human development who are honored at some sacred spots.

stillpoint. An inner place of total silence and stillness, where intuition and creativity originate and balance can be found; the source of being.

synchronicity. A term coined by the Swiss psychiatrist Carl Gustav Jung (1875-1961) defining a meaningful acausal coincidence of a psychological event and an external observable event, both taking place at or around the same time; a coincidence with meaning, seemingly beyond statistical happenstance but without a provable link.

tesseract. A hypercube, also called the 8-cell or octachoron; sacred geometry shape for ceremony, frequently depicted in art as the shape of angels.

thought forms. Organized patterns of energy, either free floating or embedded in a space, that can be broken up by rattling or other means of transmutation.

tonal. In Toltec shamanism, the idea of what is real (our common, consensus reality), in contrast to what is really real (nonordinary reality), the nagual. See nagual.

transmutation. Changing energy from one state to another, such as transforming water to ice or vapor and vice versa; changing negative, or inert, energy into positive, or active, energy; or neutralizing energy to be reabsorbed by the earth. Ancient practices involved burying an energized object in the ground, burning it with fire, or submerging it in water.

umane (Lakota: OO-Mah-ne). Sacred symbol of Earth energy in its raw form, often depicted in stone pictographs as a square with lines of energy from each corner, or as a square with enlongated corners to represent power coming from and going out to all corners of the universe.

unoli (You-know-Lee). Cherokee, meaning literally "winds" but used as a designation for the powers of the directions.

vibrational rate/vibrational frequency. The measurable level of energy of a person, place, or object; the higher the rate, the closer to the source, or optimal wholeness.

vision quest. A period of time spent in a desolate or isolated spot under the tutelage of a spiritual elder, intended as an opportunity for discovering the inner self, the meaning of life, or to connect with higher beings.

vortexes. Doorways, or portals, into other dimensions; areas where energy in flux can affect time and space.

wakan. Lakota word meaning "sacred."

Wakan-Tanka. Lakota word for Great Spirit, or the Great Mystery, God.

wand. A long, thin implement used to direct energy when pointed. Some are ornate, with carvings, feathers, beads, and similar adornments, while others are as simple as a twig or a feather.

wild spirit. A spirit of the land that usually inhabits wilderness areas away from civilization or contact with humans; ally.

will of creation. Energy of the moment, moving from one state to another; the potential to transform to another manifestation.

Bibliography

Braden, Gregg. *Awakening to Zero Point: The Collective Initiation*. Bellevue, WA: Radio Bookstore Press, 1997.

—. *Walking Between the Worlds: The Science of Compassion*. Bellevue, WA: Radio Bookstore Press, 1997.

Brueyere, Rosalyn L. *Wheels of Light: Chakras, Auras, and the Healing Energy of the Body*. New York: Simon & Schuster, 1989.

Capra, Fritjof. *The Tao of Physics*. Berkeley, CA.: Shambala, 1975.

Castaneda, Carlos. *Journey To Ixtlan: The Lessons of Don Juan*. New York: Simon & Schuster, 1977.

—. *The Teachings of Don Juan: A Yaqui Way of Knowledge*. New York: Ballantine 1973.

Catches, Pete S., Sr., Peter V. Catches, ed. Sacred Fireplace (Oceti Wakan): *Life and Teachings of a Lakota Medicine Man*. Santa Fe, NM: Clear Light Publishers, 1999.

De Garis, Hugo. *The Artilect War: Cosmists Vs. Terrans: A Bitter Controversy Concerning Whether Humanity Should Build Godlike Massively Intelligent Machines*. Palm Springs, CA: ETC Publications, 2005.

Desy, Phylameana lila. *The Everything Reiki Book: Channel Your Positive Energy to Reduce Stress, Promote Healing, and Enhance Your Quality of Life*. Cincinnati, OH: Adams Media Corporation, 2004.

Deutscher, Guy. *Through the Language Glass: Why the World Looks Different in Other Languages*. New York: Metropolitan Books, 2010.

Drake, Michael. *The Shamanic Drum: A Guide to Sacred Drumming*. Mt. Angel, OR: Talking Drum Publications, 1991.

—. *I Ching: The Tao of Drumming*. Mt. Angel, OR: Talking Drum Publications, 2003.

Eagle Feather, Ken. *A Toltec Path*. Charlottesville, VA: Hampton Roads, 1995.

—. *Toltec Dreaming: Don Juan's Teachings on the Energy Body* (Rochester, VT: Bear & Co., 2007).

Ellis, Keith. *Number Power: In Nature, Art and Everyday Life*. New York: St. Martin's, 1978.

Ewing, Jim PathFinder. *Clearing: A Guide to Liberating Energies Trapped in Buildings and Lands*. Forres, Scotland: Findhorn Press, 2006.

—. *Finding Sanctuary in Nature: Simple Ceremonies in the Native American Tradition of Healing Yourself and Others*. Forres, Scotland: Findhorn Press, 2007.

—. *Healing Plants and Animals From a Distance: Curative Principles and Applications*. Forres, Scotland: Findhorn Press, 2007.

—. *Reiki Shamanism: A Guide to Out-of-Body Healing*, Forres, Scotland: Findhorn Press, 2008.

Gaia, Laurelle Shanti. *The Book On Karuna Reiki®*. Harsel, CO: Infinite Light Healing Studies Center Inc., 2001.

Harner, Michael. *The Way of the Shaman*. New York: Harper, 1980.

Hawking, Stephen. *A Brief History of Time*. New York: Bantam, 1998.

—, and Leonard Mlodinow. *The Grand Design*. New York: Bantam, 2010.

Houston, Jean and Margaret Rubin. *Manual for the Peacemaker: An Iroquois Legend to Heal Self and Society*. New York: Quest Books, 1994.

Ingerman, Sandra. *Medicine for the Earth: How to Transform Personal and Environmental Toxins.* New York: Three Rivers Press, 2000.

—. *Shamanic Journeying: A Beginner's Guide.* Boulder, CO: Sounds True, 2004.

—. *Soul Retrieval: Mending the Fragmented Self.* San Francisco: Harper, 1991.

—. *Welcome Home: Following Your Soul's* Journey Home. San Francisco: Harper, 1993.

Kelly, Maureen J. *Reiki and the Healing Buddha.* Twin Lakes, WI: Lotus Press, 2000.

Kurzweil, Raymond. *The Singularity Is Near: When Humans Transcend Biology.* New York: Penguin, 2006.

Lungold, Ian Xel. *Mayan Calendar and Conversion Codex.* Sedona, AZ: Majix, 1999.

McElvaine, Robert S. Eve's Seed: *Biology, the Sexes and the Course of History.* New York: McGraw-Hill, 2000.

Medicine Eagle, Brooke. *The Last Ghost Dance: A Guide for Earth Mages.* New York: Wellspring/Ballantine, 2000.

—. *Buffalo Woman Comes Singing.* New York: Ballantine Books, 1991.

Melchizedek, Drunvalo. *Ancient Secrets of the Flower of Life,* vols. 1 and 2. Flagstaff, AZ: Light Technology Publishing, 1990.

Melody. *Love Is in the Earth: A Kaleidoscope of Crystals.* Wheat Ridge, CO: Earth-Love Publishing House, Ltd., 1995.

Pert, Candace B., Ph.D. *Molecules of Emotion: The Science Behind Mind-Body Medicine.* New York: Simon & Schuster, 1999.

Petter, Frank Arjava. *Reiki: The Legacy of Dr. Usui.* Twin Lakes, WI: Shangri-La Press, 1998.

—, and Dr. Mikao Usui. *The Original Reiki Handbook of Dr. Mikao Usui.* Twin Lakes, WI: Lotus Press, 1999.

Rand, William Lee. *Reiki: The Healing Touch: First and Second Degree Manual.* Southfield, MI: Vision Publications, 1991.

Redmond, Layne. *When the Drummers Were Women: A Spiritual History of Rhythm.* New York: Three Rivers Press 1997.

Rinpoche, Sogyal. *The Tibetan Book of Living and Dying.* New York: Harper, 1994.

Sambhava, Padma, and Robert A. Thurman (trans). *The Tibetan Book of the Dead.* New York: Bantam, 1994.

Taleb, Nassim Nicholas. *The Black Swan: The Impact of the Highly Improbable.* New York: Random House, 2007.

Vico, Giambattista. *The New Science of Giambattista Vico: Unabridged Translation of the Third Edition (1744) with the Addition of Practice of the New Science* (Cornell Paperbacks). Ithica, NY: Cornell University Press, 1984.

Weil, Andrew, M.D. *Sound Body, Sound Mind: Music for Healing with Dr. Andrew Weil* (Audio CD). Burbank, CA: Rhino Records, 2005.

Ywahoo, Dhyani. *Voices of the Ancestors: Cherokee Teachings from the Wisdom Fire.* Boston: Shambhala Publications, 1987.

Zukav, Gary. *The Dancing Wu Li Masters: An Overview of the New Physics.* New York: William Morrow, 1979.

About the Author

Jim PathFinder Ewing (Nvnehi Awatisgi) lives in Lena, Mississippi, where he and his wife, Annette Waya Ewing, teach classes and operate ShooFly Farm.

For more information or to subscribe to Jim's free online newsletter, *Keeping in Touch*, visit Jim and Annette's website, Healing the Earth/Ourselves, at www.blueskywaters.com. Jim is the author of:

FINDHORN PRESS

Life-Changing Books

For a complete catalogue,
please contact:

Findhorn Press
117–121 High Street
Forres IV36 1AB
Scotland, UK

t +44-(0)1309-690582
f +44-(0)131-777-2711
e info@findhornpress.com

or consult our catalogue online
(with secure order facility) on
www.findhornpress.com

For information on the Findhorn Foundation:
www.findhorn.org